THE
MARX
BROS.

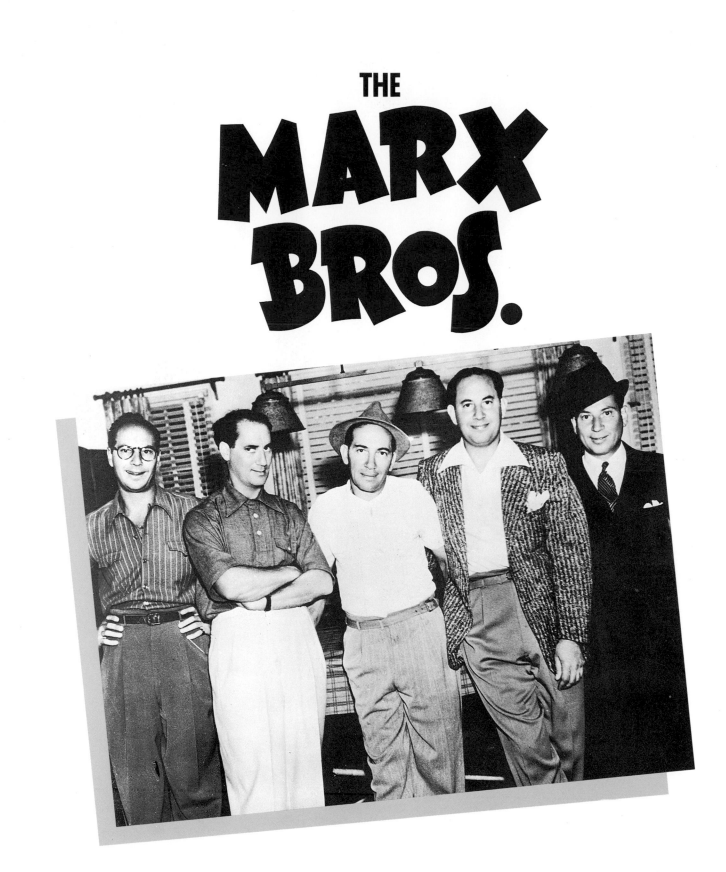

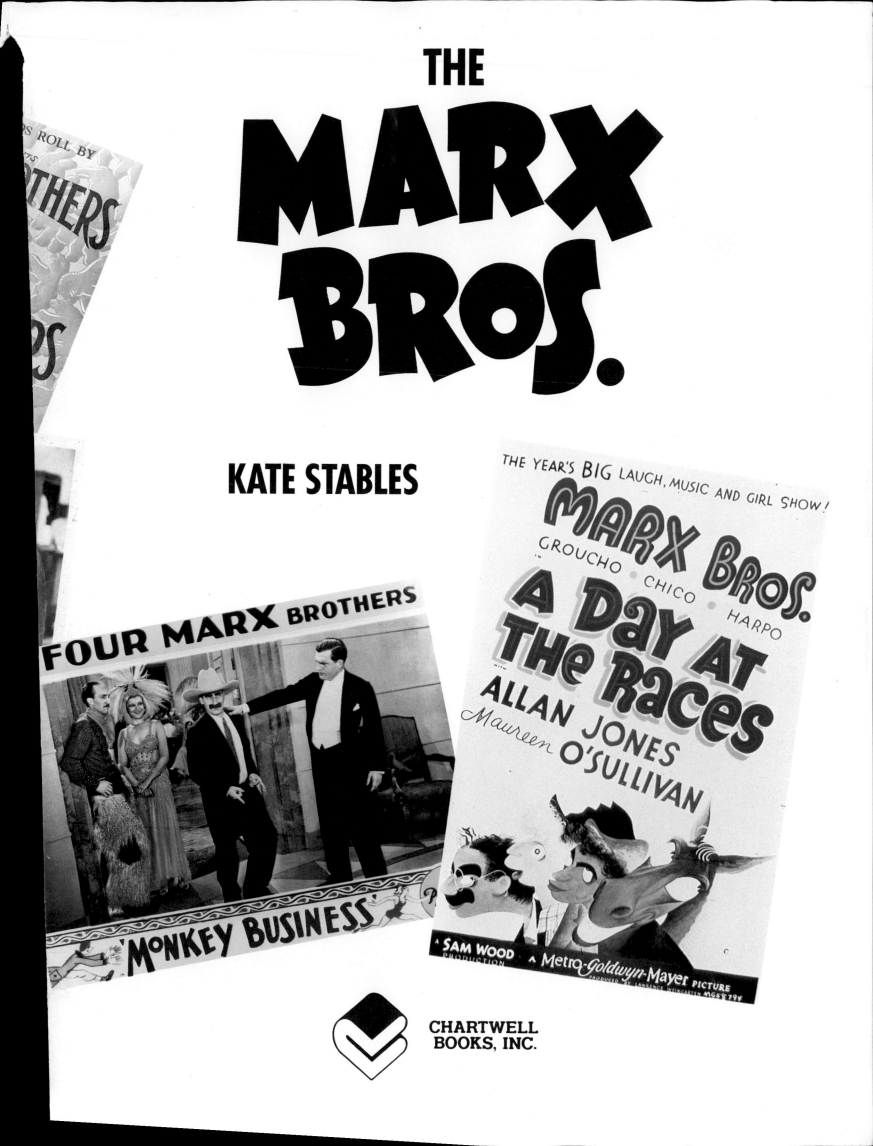

THE MARX BROS.

KATE STABLES

CHARTWELL BOOKS, INC.

Published by
CHARTWELL BOOKS, INC.
A Division of BOOK SALES, INC.
110 Enterprise Avenue
Secaucus, New Jersey 07094

Produced by
Brompton Books Corp.
15 Sherwood Place
Greenwich, CT 06830

ISBN 1-55521-793-1

Printed in Hong Kong

PAGE 1: (left to right) Zeppo, Groucho, Chico, Gummo and Harpo Marx. A rare shot of all 5 brothers together in the 1950s.

PAGE 2: (clockwise from top left) Margaret Dumont and Groucho share a tender moment in *Duck Soup* 1933); the Four Marx Brothers in their 1928 sell-out Broadway hit *Animal Crackers*; 'Gruesome isn't he' – Harpo caught red-handed in *The Big Store* (1941); Groucho gets fancy (dress) in *Monkey Business* 1931); A poster for *A Day at the Races* (1934); The Brothers are rounded up in *Go West* (1940); A publicity poster for *At the Circus* (1939)

THESE PAGES:
ABOVE: Chico and Harpo mess up a swell party in *Animal Crackers*.
ABOVE RIGHT: Groucho in vaudeville as one of *The Four Nightingales* (1909).
FAR RIGHT: Harpo, Groucho, and Chico make a hasty exit in *At the Circus*.
RIGHT: 'Making love to Mrs Claypool is my racket'; during *A Night at the Opera* (1935), Groucho plies his trade. His rival Sig Rumann is not amused.

CONTENTS

INTRODUCTION..6

CHAPTER ONE: **ROACHES IN NAGADOCHES**..........16

CHAPTER TWO: **HELLO TO HOLLYWOOD**...............28

CHAPTER THREE: **DUCK SOUP**...............................38

CHAPTER FOUR: **NIGHT AND DAY**..........................46

CHAPTER FIVE: **TIMES CHANGE**............................58

CHAPTER SIX: **FINAL BOWS**..................................66

EPILOGUE...76

INDEX...80

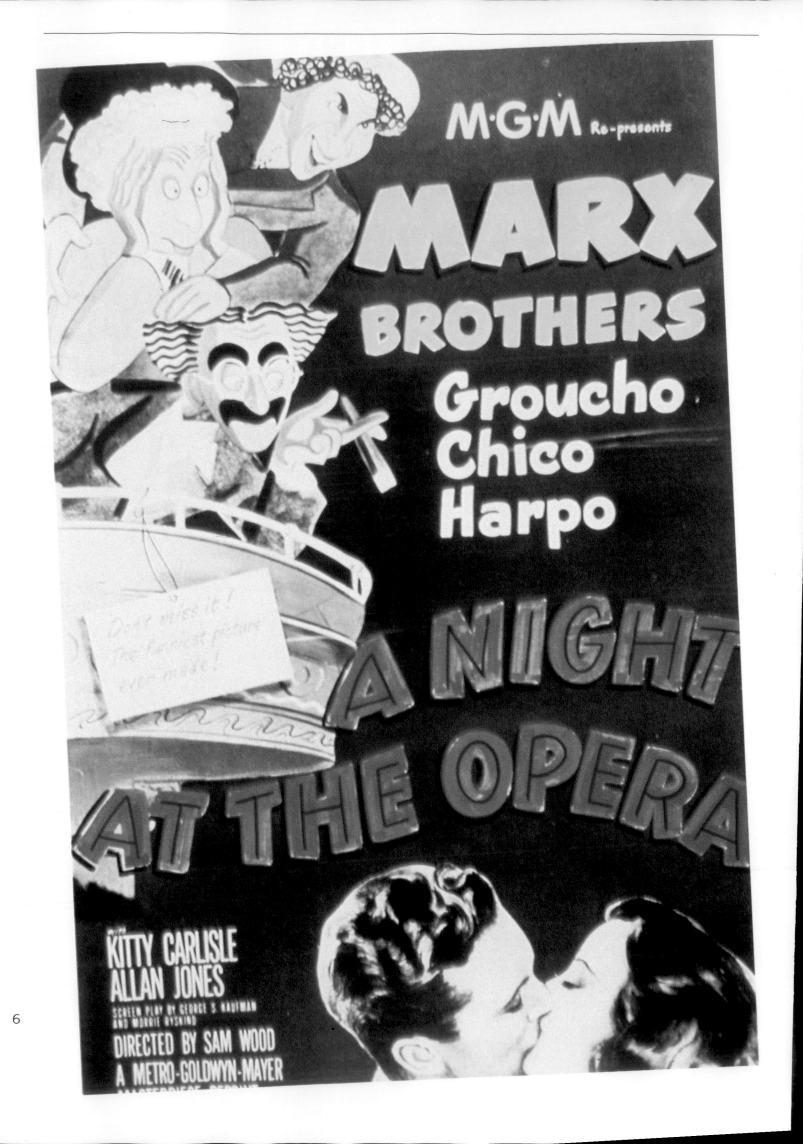

INTRODUCTION

Fame is when your name is recognized fifty years after your death. Great fame is when your face is recognized. Immortality is when you cease to be a name or a face and become a universal icon. The Marx Brothers, three immigrant vaudeville comedians with 10 years' worth of classic comedy films, are undoubtedly immortal. The mere conjunction of glasses, moustache and cigar, or a curly blond wig and top hat signals Marxian merriment to every generation around the globe.

People who have never seen their films can lope like Groucho or honk like Harpo. The wise-cracking bespectacled brother Groucho was to become the most famous of them all, closely followed by the mute angel-devil Harpo. Chico, the dialect comedian and piano player brings up the rear. In all they made only thirteen films together, of which two (*Duck Soup*, and *A Night At the Opera*) can be regarded as great, and a further three or four as classic comedies. They are the most famous comic threesome in the history of movies.

What makes them unique among classic comedians is the blend of comic skills and styles they brought to their films. Chaplin, Keaton – even Laurel and Hardy – had single comic styles, variations on the physical comedy which had been king forever. The Marx Brothers mixed several different styles of verbal comedy

(one-liners and wisecracks, whimsy and dialect humor) with sight gags and violent physical comedy. They used musical comedy (in humorous songs, and musical parodies) and clowning surreal comedy. They ignored logic and continuity and the laws of physics. So when Groucho addresses the audience directly, when costumes change from shot to shot, when a cocktail of disparate footage or trick shots is employed, the Marx Brothers are making cinematic history.

In their movies the brothers take on the world, and turn it upside down. They satirized every noble institution they could think of, from government to medicine, and every ignoble, hypocritical or pretentious behavior which accompanies them. The brothers are Lords of Misrule, upending the logical world of effort and

RIGHT: Harpo; his grandmother had been a travelling harp player in Germany.

LEFT: Mr Piano Man, Chico, shooting the breeze and the keys.

ABOVE: The Marx Brothers mix a mock milkshake in between scenes.

LEFT: The Brothers combine business and pleasure with their secretary at MGM, their new home from 1935.

ABOVE RIGHT: Sig Rumann at Harpo's mercy at the climax of *A Night at the Opera*; Chico and Groucho study the sanity clause, left.

RIGHT: Horse doctor Dr Hackenbush (Groucho) treats his first (nearly) human patient in *A Day at the Races*.

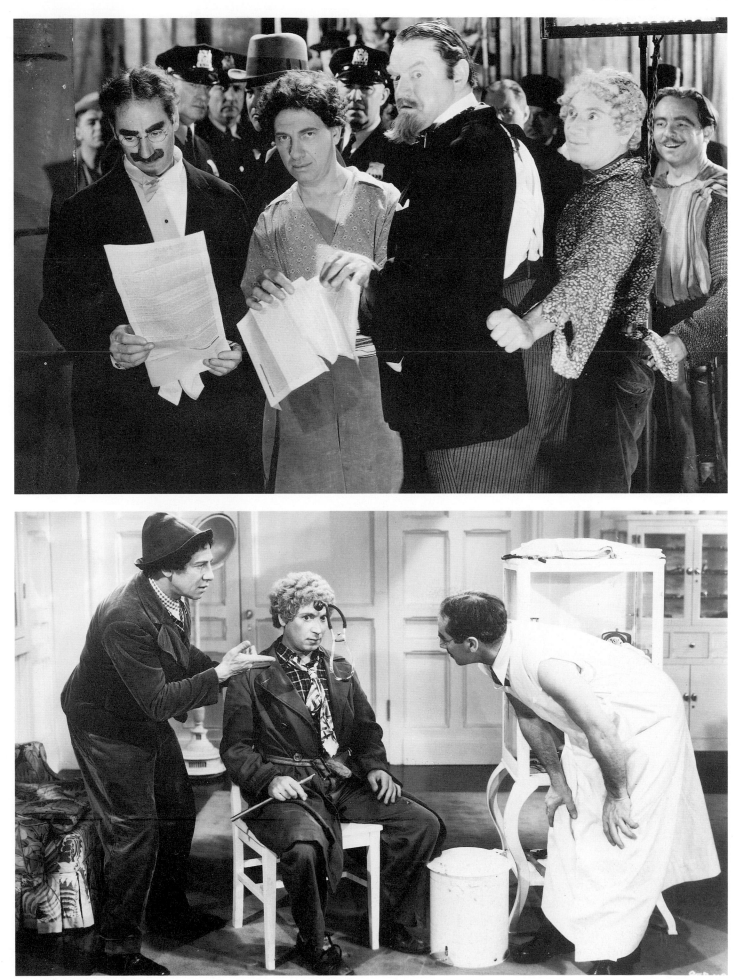

Alexander Woollcott, George Bernard Shaw, Salvador Dali, TS Eliot and Winston Churchill among their greatest contemporary fans. They were the brightest stars of the 1920s on Broadway, and their zany satires fit the 1930s to a 't'. They were a Hollywood institution in the 1940s, canonized by TV in the 1950s and rediscovered in the 1960s and 1970s. Throughout the 1980s any Marx Brothers' movie in repertory cinema or TV schedule was a sure audience winner. From the 1990s, with their classic canon available on video, they will be always with us.

Age cannot wither them, nor custom stale their infinite variety. For the Marx Brothers, immortality is not enough, they also demand celebration, and this book is an attempt to do just that.

ABOVE: Art imitates life; Chico ponders his next move at the card table in *Animal Crackers*.

ABOVE RIGHT: Miss Marlowe, to rhyme with Harlow; Esther Muir decorated both poster and movie of *A Day at the Races*.

RIGHT: Blame it on the bellboys; the Brothers mug in a publicity shot for RKO's 1938 *Room Service*.

CHAPTER ONE: **ROACHES IN NAGADOCHES**

They started their screen career as The Four Marx Brothers; in fact there were five surviving sons born to Minnie and Sam Marx. Naming all five has become a favorite trivial pursuit – Chico, Harpo, Groucho, Zeppo ... and Gummo. Minnie's Boys they started out, and Minnie's Boys they would always be. Minnie Marx, indefatigable mother and agent, was responsible not only for bringing them into the world but also for unleashing them on show business. Arriving in America in the early 1880s Minnie Schoenberg, a Jewish immigrant from Bavaria, married Sam Marx. If she was not exactly born in a trunk,

LEFT: Minnie Marx, 'mother of the two-a-day', as a young girl. Her sons gave all their daughters names starting with M, as a tribute to her.

RIGHT: Chico (second from right) and a bashful four-year-old Groucho (back) with their cousins. Despite his later image, Groucho was always the most introspective brother.

Minnie had showbusiness in her blood. Back home in Germany her father had been a travelling musician and ventriloquist, while her mother played the harp. She helped her brother Al break into vaudeville, by badgering booking agents on his behalf, and when the aimiable Sam proved to be better at pinochle than his professed trade of tailoring, she took over responsibility for the family fortunes.

While her brother became the celebrated vaudeville star Al Shean, Minnie and Sam became parents, first of Leonard (Chico), born 1887 with his mother's energy and charm, and then of Adolph, born in 1888 and blessed with his father's dreamy creative streak. Although later officially Arthur, he was never called anything except Harpo, even by his family. The two brothers looked very much alike. Indeed, in later life Chico would seduce women, claiming to be Harpo. Julius Henry (Groucho) was born in 1890, clever and anxious from the first; good-natured Milton (Gummo) arrived in 1893, with baby Herbert (Zeppo) in 1901, last in life as he was on screen.

The Marx boys grew up primarily on East 93rd Street on the upper East Side of New York City, living with their grandfather Lafe Schoenberg. Grandfather entertained Harpo with magic tricks, and family legend has it that Harpo acquired his first harp from his grandmother, though it is more likely that it was provided by Uncle Al, the family member who could best afford it. This glamorous uncle was a popular childhood visitor; in the early years of the century he was one of the most highly paid vaudeville performers around, as part of the comedy and musical act The Manhattan Comedy Four.

Minnie was determined to get her children into showbusiness. Her first experiments were on the fifteen-year-old Groucho, a stage-struck boy soprano who was first integrated into and then abandoned on tour by The Leroy Trio, and then similarly treated by a series of musical acts from 1905 through 1907. Finally that year Minnie took matters into her own hands and set him up with Gummo and a wall-eyed soprano, Mabel O'Donnell, as a musical trio, the Four Nightingales. Their friend Lou Levy suc-

ceeded Mabel O'Donnell in 1908, as Minnie Marx continued to hawk them mercilessly to vaudeville bookers as an opening act.

When she added the hapless Harpo later on that year the act became the Four Nightingales, and it was in this guise that they toured some of the toughest vaudeville halls going. When by 1910 they had exhausted the New York area, Minnie moved the whole family to Chicago, where the vaudeville circuit was flourishing if rough, and, more importantly the act was unknown.

There seems to be no doubt that vaudeville forged the Marx Brothers' distinctive style. Though billed as a musical act, they

ABOVE: A baby-faced Zeppo, aged 11, the youngest Marx brother. At 17 he was touring the Chicago circuit with the act.

RIGHT: The Four Nightingales: (left to right) Gummo, Leo Levin, Groucho, Harpo. Gummo was replaced by Zeppo in 1919.

took to joking and roughhousing as a survival tactic onstage. Groucho's son, Arthur, tells how when a runaway mule in Nagodoches, Texas, spirited their audience outside, the Brothers ran amok, insulting the audience with puns like 'Nagadoches is full of roaches,' and happily regained their attention. This sowed the seeds for the Brothers' famous stage and screen anarchy. The hard school of provincial vaudeville taught them three things about the act: keep it fresh; keep it frantic; keep the audience.

It was during this period of their vaudeville career that they became fully fledged comics. Though they had started as a musical act with humor, when they took to joking and fooling around on stage as a survival tactic, the act became comedy with music, rather than vice-versa, and in 1910, they started touring with a school skit, 'Fun in Hi Skule.' These had been popularized by comic Gus Edwardes, and were a weather-proof crowd pleaser. The act was enlivened by anarchic disregard for the script, violent chasing and roughhousing, and a galloping tendency to ad-lib, which could be corrected only by the presence of Minnie hissing the name of the man holding the mortgage on their Chicago house!

Frank Hauser, reviewing their earlier years in 1951, wondered when 'talent began to settle on them like dust,' as it

arx Bros.

hadn't been notable during their earliest years on the boards. The answer might lie in this skit, in which we find the first signs of later characters familiar to millions of movie-goers. Groucho played a wisecracking teacher with a German accept (a characteristic which was dropped at the outbreak of World War I). Gummo was a foil, the standard Jewish schoolboy, with Harpo as Patsy Branni-gan, the Irish school-idiot. Chico, who had had a small and slightly classier career as a piano accompanist in vaude-ville and for silent films, decided to join the act in 1912, bringing his Italian-dialect comedy with him.

'Fun in Hi Skule' was popular with audiences, but unpopular with manage-ment because of its wild attitude and antics. Fellow perfomers were terrified to follow the Brothers on stage. WC Fields, whose career (starting as a juggler in vaudeville) closely mimicked that of the Brothers, once told Chico's daughter Maxine that he faked a broken arm rather than follow them on stage since they literally wrecked the theater.

When this act wore out its welcome, Uncle Al Shean, enjoying a second suc-cess as with Ed Gallagher as the famous 'Positively Mr Gallagher, Absolutely Mr Shean,' knocked them up a skit called

ABOVE: Mamma's Boys; (left to right) Harpo, Groucho, and Gummo on the Vaudeville circuit in 1908.

RIGHT: The Four Nightingales: (from top) Groucho, Harpo, Gummo, and Leo Levin. Note Harpo's strong resemblance to Chico; they were often mistaken for one another off-stage.

'Home Again,' which was the first Marx Brothers' vehicle to combine all the elements of their later shows. It gave Groucho abundant wise-cracks as Mr Schneider, a prosperous businessman disembarking from a sea voyage, who is bothered by crafty Italian immigrant Chico, and savage-mute Harpo. This came about because Al Shean, in his haste, had forgotten to give Harpo any lines, and soothed him by turning him into a European-style silent clown and, inadvertently, a comic legend.

The second half was a society party as the Schnieder's (a location which was to be the basis for several Marx classics, including *Animal Crackers, Duck Soup*, and *At the Circus*), where Groucho joins in Harpo and Chico's disruptive antics, Gummo played straightman as Groucho's son, but was replaced by Zeppo when he was drafted into World War I in 1917. By this point the Brothers had acquired their distinctive stage uniforms: Groucho had glasses and moustache, to make him look older, while Harpo sported a red wig, battered hat, and bottomless raincoat, complete with hooter. Chico was already in the folkloric Italian Alp costume which would last throughout his career.

It was while touring with 'Home Again' in 1914 that the Marx Brothers acquired their stage names. These became, perversely, their 'real' names by which they would be known to family, friends, and fans alike. They were bestowed during a poker-game with monologist Art Fisher. Groucho got his name either for his pessimism or after the grouch (money) bag which vaudevillians wore; Harpo, rather obviously, for his harp; Gummo for his rubber galoshes and Chico (Chicko) for his womanizing. Die-hard Marx fans spot interlopers by the widespread, but erroneous Italian pronounciation of his nickname. No accounts agree on why Zeppo came by his name, apart from its chiming with his brothers'.

'Home Again' served the Brothers well and after a more ambitious show had failed to take root ('The Street Cinderella' of 1918), it was only supplanted in 1921 by a novelty piece called 'On the Mezzanine Floor,' which combined the Marx Brothers with heavyweight-title holder Benny Leonard.

ABOVE LEFT: 'Positively Mr Gallagher, Absolutely Mr Shean;' Ed Gallagher and (right) the Brothers' uncle, Al Shean, at the height of their fame.

ABOVE: The Man Who Came to Dinner: Alexander Woollcott, broadway critic and author was the first to champion the Marx Brothers.

LEFT: Gummo, Groucho (standing), and Harpo. Uncle Julius Schickler, for whom Groucho was named, is center.

Chico, the most ambitious of the Brothers, had his sights set on Broadway, and got them there after a disagreement with the circuit-owner E F Albee black-listed them in vaudeville. Desperate after the rival Schubert circuit folded, Chico, who had been acting as their manager since his incorporation into the act, stumbled on a backer. Pretzel-manufacturer Hermann Broody was willing to trade backing for a new show in exchange for a role for his girlfriend. The show they concocted from two failed shows, 'Love For Sale' and 'Give Me A Thrill,' was a revue, with the vaguely insulting title 'I'll Say She Is.' 'Revue,' which was one up from 'vaudeville,' just as 'vaudeville' was one up from 'burlesque,' was a catch-all term for some well-worn-in Marx Brothers material, some new gags, old scenery, and dancing girls.

After an 18-month tour and a surprisingly good summer season in Philadelphia, they opened at the Casino Theater in May 1924. The second half of the show contained a bedroom scene which had all the hallmarks of their later work. Groucho played Napoleon, saying repeated goodbyes to a nymphomaniac Josephine, unaware that his fellow generals (played by Chico and Harpo) are hidden in the room waiting their turn. By happy accident, the heavyweight New York critics were in attendance on the first night, after the opening of a more dignified play had been postponed at short notice. The Marx Brothers' potent cocktail of slapstick, clowning, and high-speed wisecracks went rapidly to the critics' heads and the Brothers garnered rave reviews. Alexander Woollcott, humorist and critic of the New York *Sun*, became a life-long fan and champion of the Brothers, celebrating them (and Harpo especially) in essays, and introducing them to the celebrated Algonquin Round Table.

The Brothers became the toast of New York, and topped 'I'll Say She Is' in 1925 with *The Cocoanuts*, a satire on the Florida land-boom, and their first narrative comedy. George S Kaufman, the most sought-after comic playwright of the 1920s, had been brought in by producer Sam Harris. Kaufman (author of *Once in A Lifetime*, and winner of the Pulitzer prize for *Of Thee I Sing*) was, with co-author Morrie Ryskind, to be responsible for much of the Marx Brothers' greatest work. The music for *The Cocoanuts* was by Irving Berlin, presumably on an off-day, since it is completely unmemorable. Groucho plays the owner of a Florida hotel disrupted by deadbeats Chico and Harpo. The plot, such as it is, concerns the efforts of Mr Hammer (Groucho) to sell lots in Cocoanut Grove, while making outrageous overtures to wealthy widow Mrs Potter. Mrs Potter's daughter Polly is in love with young architect Bob Adams, who is working as a hotel clerk. When Mrs Potter's diamond necklace is stolen, Bob Adams is implicated and imprisoned. Harpo, as ever the improbable hero of the film, restores the necklace to Mrs Potter, and frees Bob.

But the real thieves are Harvey Yates, a Boston con-man and his side-kick Penelope. Yates is set to marry Polly, but at a fancy dress party that evening to celebrate their engagement, the Brothers unmask the real villains.

23

Another landmark talent acquisition for the Brothers was Margaret Dumont, who made her debut here with them as Mrs Potter. The widow of a Social Register businessman, she was perfectly cast as the dowager, stately as a galleon, and about as cognisant about comedy. The Brothers abused her savagely on- and off-stage, but she provided them with the ballast they needed and stuck with them throughout their movie career, eventually being hailed as 'the Fifth Marx Brother.'

The show was daring and sophisticated and once again a smash-hit. The Marx Brothers were now firmly established as the roaring hit of Roaring Twenties' New York. *The Cocoanuts* stayed on Broadway until 1928, a feat of milking

LEFT: Pulitzer Prize-winning playwright George S Kaufman. He was responsible for some of the Marx Brothers' greatest work, but their incessant ad-libs infuriated him.

BELOW LEFT: The Brothers in a typically 'natural' pose from *The Cocoanuts* ((1929).

BELOW: Harpo, complete with dark red wig, and Chico (sporting vaudeville greasepaint eyebrows) attempt to spring hero Oscar Shaw in *The Cocoanuts*.

made possible by the fact that the show was varied endlessly by the Brothers' ad-libbing – a vaudeville habit ingrained from years of touring – which prolonged the show's life with repeat business. There is a legendary story that George Kaufman once silenced a companion backstage with 'Hush. I thought I heard one of the original lines of the show.'

Kaufman came back for more punishment, however, with *Animal Crackers*, a high-society satire which was to provide Groucho with his theme song 'Hooray For Captain Spaulding,' written by Bert Kalmar and Harry Ruby (who went on to write both scripts and songs for the Marx Brothers most successful films, as well as penning such classics as 'Who's Sorry Now'). Groucho, posing as Captain Spaulding, the brave explorer ('Did someone call me schnorrer?') is feted at a society house-party given by Mrs Rittenhouse, while Chico and Harpo run amok. *Animal Crackers* sold out on opening night, and gave the Brothers their third hit in a row.

While still the toast of Broadway, the Marx Brothers had embarked upon their first film, transferring *The Cocoanuts* to film by day, while playing *Animal Crackers* at night. Filming took place at Paramount's Long Island studios, and was beset by the endless technical problems common to early talking pictures, the erratic behavior of the Brothers, and a director (Robert Florey) who had very little control over them or their work. In fact this talkie was the Brothers second film. They had financed, shot, and quickly buried a 1920 silent short called *Humorisk*.

The Cocoanuts is rarely screened today – the sound quality of the prints is poor, and frankly so is the technical execution of the film. Marx Brothers critics prize it mostly as a faithful record of the stage show, complete with stocky chorus lines of high-kicking pagegirls and bathers, and for its glints of comic gold – Groucho spooning with Margaret Dumont with a sewer pipe, for instance, and the Groucho-Chico 'Why-a-Duck' map exchange. The humor (if not the narrative) stands the test of time better than many pallid Broadway contemporaries, but its real interest is in showing how highly developed the Marx Brothers were with their own unique brand of comedy. The exchanges have a kind of snap and vulgarity ('Your eyes, they shine like the pants of my blue serge suit') which was new in films dominated hitherto by a very broad and often sentimental physical comedy.

The Cocoanuts includes singing lovebirds Mary Eaton and Oscar Shaw (a precursor of MGM packages to come) and the musical solos which had become a staple in the Marx Brothers' work since vaudeville for Chico and Harpo. Viewed nowadays, it is a curious mixture of fully-finished Marx madness (Groucho and Harpo, in particular, are indistinguishable from their later screen selves) and Twenties' camp. In addition, there are in-

numerable bits of business which were to crop up again in their later work (Harpo eating objects off the Reception desk and a connecting-bedroom chase which heralds *A Night at The Opera*).

The fall of 1929 brought bad news to mar that year's triple glories of a hit film, hit show, and a brief vaudeville triumph at the Palace Theater in New York. Minnie Marx died in September of a cerebral haemorrhage, but not before she had witnessed her sons' film success. Shortly afterwards Groucho and Harpo lost around a quarter of a million dollars apiece in the Wall Street Crash.

After the success of *The Cocoanuts*, Paramount were quick to commit *Animal Crackers* to film the following year. Again shot in Long Island, and once more a close cinematic copy of the stage show, this time the Marx Brothers were prevented from unpunctuality, absenteeism or group bad behavior by the mildly inhumane but effective ploy of (literally) caging them separately. Director Victor Heerman (a veteran of Mack Sennett's

studios) had four boxes constructed on set, in which the Brothers were incarcerated by four assistant directors, whose sole purpose was to keep them on the set and out of mischief. This device made for a firmer grip all around – the technical advances of a year in 'talkie' movie making were significant, if not considerable, the performances have a more confident feel and the hit and miss humour of *The Cocoanuts*, with as many flubs as zingers, is replaced by a pacier, crisper humor all round.

Animal Crackers, though sometimes considered inferior to *The Cocoanuts* in the quality over quantity reckoning, has much more Marx Brothers to the mix than its predecessor and is by far the best known of the early pictures. This is partly from Groucho's attachment to the Captain Spaulding character, and also down to the high quotient of memorable gags. Probably the best known is Groucho's 'One morning I shot an elephant in my pajamas. How he got in my pajamas I don't know.'

BELOW: The Great Dictator: Groucho threatens Zeppo in front of society hostess Mrs Rittenhouse (Margaret Dumont). Zeppo's backchat here, unusually, upstages Groucho.

The plot doesn't bear very close inspection. Captain Spaulding's visit is interrupted by the theft of Mrs Rittenhouse's Beauregard painting. But it was the first Marx Brothers film to feature a setting and sequences consistently worthy of satire. Zeppo makes one of his most memorable appearances in *Animal Crackers*, sweetening up the crowd for the legendary Captain, and he bites back at Groucho with some delightful deadpan in the dictation scene ('Now you said a lot of things here that I didn't think were important so I just omitted them').

Chico is also properly integrated as a musician summoned to play for the party (Groucho: 'Signor Ravelli's first selection is "Somewhere My Love Lies Sleeping" with a male chorus'). He informs Captain Spaulding that his fees are on a sliding scale — if he doesn't play at all, they won't be able to afford him. He assists Harpo in the most violent comedy ever seen in their work - the scene in which Harpo challenges Mrs Rittenhouse to a fight and punches her viciously, if theatrically,

before settling down to a childishly outrageous bout of cheating at cards.

Unlike their silent-film predecessors, Laurel and Hardy and the Keystone Kops, the Marx Brothers made very little use of blunt physical attack in their work. Most demolition is verbal, with Groucho slicing and dicing with an effortless aristry. His victims are both women ('You have got money haven't you? Because if you haven't we can quit right now') and, even more unsubtly, men ('How much would you charge to throw yourself down an open manhole?')

Animal Crackers joins the handful of early talkies which can still attract an audience today, an extraordinary achievement for a film which started life on stage in 1929. It is as irreverent today as at was on release ('Africa is God's country — and He can have it') and it's success opened new doors for the Marx Brothers. In the words of their 1940 comedy, Paramount invited them to 'Go West.' So, in 1931 the Brothers said byebye to Broadway and hello to Hollywood.

BELOW: *Animal Crackers* (1930). The society-party setting became a Marx Brothers staple.

THE MARX BROTHERS

"THE COCOANUTS" are up to "Monkey Business." Reading from left to right, they are, Chico, Harpo, Groucho and Zeppo. The Marx Brothers always sign their contracts in green ink and like to have the soles of their feet tickled

RAY JONES

CHAPTER TWO: **HELLO TO HOLLYWOOD**

By 1931 the Marx Brothers were the veterans of two screen-comedy successes, and 25 years apiece in vaudeville. The logical move was to Hollywood, where the weather was warmer, the best movie talent congregated, and Paramount beckoned. The Marx Brothers' family entourage made the move lock, stock, and barrel, transporting with them their delighted father, Sam, and a selection of New York's finest writing talent for their next picture. Notable among these was SJ Perelman, wit, humorist, and, alongside the Brothers, an American institution. He is generally credited with a distinctive stamp on the original screenplays of *Monkey Business* and, to a lesser degree, its successor *Horse Feathers*.

Monkey Business was to be the Marx Brothers' first original film comedy, and like many first-borns, it had a troubled birth and traumatic childhood. Perelman and collaborator Will B Johnstone (a veteran of 'I'll Say She Is') had a basic premise. Their notion of four shipboard stowaways was then pushed, pulled, and re-worked by a procession of writers added to and aided by the Marx Brothers. These included Arthur Sheekman (Groucho's gagman), novice Nat Perrin and a bemused cartoonist called J Carver

Pusey whose brief was to create sight gags for Harpo. SJ Perelman later observed that 'anybody who ever worked on any picture for the Marx Brothers said he would rather be chained to a galley oar and lashed at ten minute intervals than ever work for those sons of bitches again.'

The Brothers had a stroke of luck with their producer, the larger-than-life Herman Mankiewicz, brother of the more famous Joseph. A hugely talented writer and wit himself (he wrote the screenplay for *Citizen Kane*, and was heard to remark 'There, but for the grace of God, goes God' as Orson Welles passed), Mankiewicz practiced a kind of benign neglect with the Brothers and director Norman Macleod. That he not only understood the Brothers' unique humor but also shared it can be gleaned from the fact that he was the only man ever to write a Rin Tin Tin script in which the dog took a baby *into* a burning house . . .

The plot that they wound up with is the only one to feature the Brothers as a unit from word one. The Brothers are discovered stowing away in the hold in kippered-herring barrels. 'I know there's four of them because they're singing

ABOVE LEFT: A barrel of laughs; a barber-shop quartet for the hard of hearing in *Monkey Business*.

LEFT: S J Perelman; wit, humorist and reluctant Marx collaborator.

ABOVE: Behind You! The stowaways hide out from the Captain and his men onboard ship in *Monkey Business*.

Sweet Adeline' the First Officer remarks (although how he knows about Harpo, who can only mouth, we'll never know). Chased out into the open, the Brothers run rings around the crew and the deck. After a sustained tease in which Groucho and Chico bamboozle the captain and steal his lunch, the boys crash staterooms at random, and wind up as two pairs of impromptu bodyguards to rival gangsters, Alky Briggs (played with serious intent by Harry Woods) and Joe Helton (George Raft lookalike, Rockliffe Fellowes).

Romance has entered the lives of two of the Brothers, as Groucho tangoes passionately with Lucille Briggs, Alky's frustrated wife, and Zeppo makes the acquaintance of Mary, Helton's daughter. Halfway through the society party which Helton throws for his daughter to mark her return to the States, Mary is kidnapped and taken to the Old Barn by Alky and his men. The Marx Brothers abandon their disruption of the party to find and save her.

Just as *Animal Crackers* took a poke at the gullibility of high society, so *Monkey Business* satirizes the business of ship-board etiquette, and gangsters, both real and cinematic. Alky Briggs is the very model of a big-talking cinema gangster, where Joe Helton, who is hell-bent on integrating himself and his daughter into the respectable world, prompts a satire on the assimilating of gangsters into polite society.

Monkey Business marks several small but notable changes in style for the Brothers. The film's action is relentlessly mobile, and the gags are razor sharp. Because the Brothers are outcasts, the exchanges with authority and assaults on passing human targets get some snap, crackle, and pop going. Where *Animal Crackers* had Groucho accepted by the house-party so that his rallies of nonsense and insult were often met by a sort of blank tolerance or indulgent smiles, here we really feel that the Brothers are getting a rise out of their targets.

The end result is a stand-alone comedy without any of the stagey 1920s' trappings of *The Cocoanuts* or *Animal Crackers*. *Monkey Business*, along with *Duck Soup*, has a distinct schoolboy cleverness. When gangster Briggs tells Groucho he is wise to him, the retort is

31

ABOVE LEFT: Groucho lays siege to college widow Connie Bailey (Thelma Todd) in *Horse Feathers* (1932). Chico is the meat in the sandwich.

LEFT: Chico and Harpo sign on as bodyguards to Joe Helton (Rockliffe Fellowes, far right) in *Monkey Business*. Yes it's a gun, and no he's not pleased to see you . . .

ABOVE: Harpo and a couple of four-legged friends in *Horse Feathers*.

'Wise eh? What's the capital of Nebraska? What's the capital of the Chase National Bank?.' The plot is possibly the thinnest of any Marx Brothers movie – those who like their comedy undisturbed by narrative concerns traditionally rate this film highly.

To a 1990s' audience the film has a more modern feel than many of its successors, often from its unusually literate dialogue ('Come Kapelmeister, let the violas throb, my regiment leaves at dawn,' a line which parodies the popular Von Stroheim epics of the time). The script has an all-round zaniness which incorporates the surreal (Harpo turning into a Punch and Judy puppet to escape the second officer), the shocking (Groucho to Thelma Todd: 'Madam, before I get through with you, you will have a clear case for divorce, and so will my wife'), and some old-fashioned tomfoolery (Chico and Harpo destroying an officer's moustache in the barber's chair).

Director Norman MacLeod mixes long-established Marx Brothers' specialities (the Groucho/Chico music-hall exchange over a globe: 'That's a shortcut' 'Strawberry shortcake?') with some new gags exclusive to film which were to reappear elsewhere. The Brothers' tableau in steamer chairs on the deck (Harpo hides under two other people while Chico impersonates a shy maiden), will be echoed later in Harpo hiding in Edgar Kennedy's bath in *Duck Soup* and is the forerunner of the fabulous three-into-two armchair deception of *A Night at The Opera*.

Horse Feathers, the college comedy which was next off the blocks in 1932, can be bracketted with *Monkey Business* by reason of its pedigree (Norman McLeod directing again) and Perelman's and Johnstone's involvement in the script, which was largely devised in this instance by Bert Kalmar and Harry Ruby. It shares the same wacky tone and to-hell-with-it comedy as *Monkey Business*, but with a broader, burlesque feel and a more highly developed plot. The comedy, oddly enough for a college satire, is more juvenile and less pointed than in *Monkey Business*, with a fair amount of sight-gags and physical comedy, particularly in the football-field and kidnapping scenes. The only nod to higher education is in the names of the two colleges – Darwin and Huxley were famous intellectual rivals in Victorian England. But really, Harpo shows the film's contempt for education by shovelling books into the fire in Groucho's study.

Kalmar and Ruby opt for poking riotous and unlikely fun at college life. Critics remarked that it was a college satire put together by people who had never gone to college, and the comedy is much more concerned with college football than poking explicit fun at higher education.

The film covers the brief and unlikely reign at stuffy Huxley College of Professor Wagstaff (Groucho). We open on his inauguration and follow his quest to rescue his son Frank (played by Zeppo, extraordinarily diffidently even for Zeppo) from the college widow – by the ingenious method of spooning with her himself. His other task is to save the college football team by stocking it with 'ringers,' recruited via a downtown speakeasy, and winning the big game.

There are broad hints at the Marxs' vaudeville background throughout the movie. None more so than the lecture scene in which Groucho attempts to teach biology to a restless Chico and Harpo, who employ everything from girlie posters ('Take that to my bedroom immediately!') to brawling. They finally lure Groucho out of teacher mode and into a fixed battle with peashooters. This is a direct throwback to 'Fun in Hi Skule,' in which the Brothers even reprise their old roles.

As so often with the Marx Brothers, the opening scene is a gem. It's full of incongruities (Groucho a college President!) and belly laughs. And, of course, it sets the scene, this time with the nonsense song 'Whatever it is, I'm Against it', which Groucho performs with a burlesque gusto which would have done credit to his Uncle Al Shean. He is supported by a bemused but docile chorus of bearded professors who dance round the table obediently in his wake, like a cross between a Jewish wedding and a minstrel revue. There is an echo of *Animal Crackers* here as the Brothers' victims are carried along by, rather than fuming at, their antics.

Another scene which was emerging as a Marx Brothers' staple was the bedroom scene, in this instance simultaneously suggestive (Groucho to Connie Bailey: 'You're ruining that boy. Why can't you do as much for me?'), insulting ('You've got more students than the college'), and downright crowded. Here the unfaithful Connie Bailey (Thelma Todd) is squeezed and set upon by a trio of Marx Brothers, as Chico and Harpo sprint through Groucho's seduction scene with ice and lame excuses, culminating in a human sandwich.

The big finale is for once outdoors, rather than the party or showdown setting which characterizes so much of their work. Opinion is divided over its merits. Some Marx lovers find it insufficiently distinctive. It doesn't feature a stuffy setting to be uproariously disrupted but is a straightforward comic take-off of college football. The Brothers set off gags like fireworks – Chico and Harpo playing cards in the middle of a scrum, Groucho's joke commentary, Harpo's triumphant entrance in a garbage chariot.

Though *Horse Feathers* uses a broader brush than its predecessor, some of the nicest moments are small ones. Chico denies Groucho access to a speakeasy, until their nonsense exchange has run its course. The password is the name of a fish; Groucho guesses sturgeon, Chico is amazed: 'Hey you crazy? Sturgeon's a doctor, cuts you open when you're sick.' This routine is one which appears in several of their films in which the plot demands that Groucho tax Chico for something; we know that they will both get what they want in the end, but we love to see them get there.

Harpo is, for once, gainfully employed: he is a dogcatcher, harassed by policeman, whom he incarcerates in his van and offers for sale. He is also an unabashed pickpocket, who enjoys a lucky streak (telephones and fruit machines vomit money for him). In addition Harpo has a trio of memorable gags which are all visual puns – producing a sword on a fish for the password 'swordfish,' dancing a highland reel for a Scotch, and taking an axe to a pack of cards on the command 'cut.'

When the Brothers have won the football game by dint of outrageous cheating

LEFT: Bound for glory: the Brothers rouse the Huxley College football team in *Horse Feathers*.

BELOW LEFT: The Boys in an exceptionally stagey publicity photo (even for them) for *Horse Feathers*.

BELOW: The boys make their mark with Sid Grauman, outside his Chinese Theater in Hollywood in 1932.

(justified since Darwin fielded professional players), the film saves a playfully immoral sting for the tail when Groucho, Chico, and Harpo are married polygamously to Connie Bailey. Ironically, it was rumoured that Zeppo was in real life having an affair with Thelma Todd, proving that in real life he didn't always get the sticky end of the lollipop.

Horse Feathers was a commercial success, with its knockabout mainstream humour, but met with less critical applause than *Monkey Business*. The Brothers, nonetheless, made the cover of *Time* magazine, and embarked on a new venture when Groucho and Chico premiered their first radio show in November 1932.

It was *Flywheel, Shyster, and Flywheel* sponsored by Essolube on NBC (the original title of *Beagle, Shyster and Beagle* fell victim to the complaints of a lawyer called Beagle). Groucho played a shyster lawyer and Chico his bumbling assistant. The gags were cornier than ever:

> GROUCHO: I've had a big day in court.
>
> ASSISTANT: What was the case?
>
> GROUCHO: Disorderly conduct, but I think I'll get off.

The show, much of it's contents scavenged from *The Cocoanuts* and *Animal Crackers*, was only reasonably successful due to its early time slot and the Brothers were not renewed for a second season. In retrospect we should be thankful for this. Both Chico and Groucho would have been unlikely to return to movie making if they had landed a long-running radio show, as radio was a well-paid and cushy number compared to shooting movies.

Duck Soup was in preparation in Hollywood, however, and the Four Marx Brothers reunited for what turned out to be their last and best film as a quartet, and their final film for Paramount.

CHAPTER THREE: **DUCK SOUP**

Duck Soup started life as a genre parody; Paramount studio-boss Ernst Lubitsch was to direct the Brothers in a Ruritanian spoof of his own work. It wound up as a genre classic. It is considered to be one of the best comedy films ever made, along with Keaton's *The General* and Chaplin's *The Gold Rush*.

It is the only Marx Brothers' film which boasted a director with a considerable career of his own. Leo McCarey, whom the Brothers had requested, had made his name with Hal Roach, as the man who

brought together Laurel and Hardy and as the director of their *Big Business*. He was to go on to win Oscars for *The Awful Truth* and *Going my Way*, the last being one of the 'sentimental Catholic Comedies' for which he was to be known in the 1940s.

In truth, *Duck Soup* is not typical of McCarey's work. It is definitively a Marx Brothers' picture and McCarey's contributions to it have more to do with his earlier Laurel and Hardy experience than his character comedies to come. He was responsible for the famous 'mirror'

LEFT: Harpo goes out with a bang in the ammunition cupboard in *Duck Soup* (1933).

BELOW: The Freedonian Freedom fighters ready to repel boarders in *Duck Soup*.

LEFT: 'All God's chillun got guns:' the boys whipping up a patriotic frenzy in *Duck Soup*.

RIGHT: Groucho orders out, during the battle scene in *Duck Soup*. His changing uniforms show a blatant disregard for film continuity.

sequence (of which more later) which sprang from his silent-comedy love of sight gags. He was also responsible for the peanut-stand versus lemonade-vendor feud which runs through the middle of the film as a microcosm of the larger, diplomatic argument going on between Freedonia and Sylvania.

Duck Soup is a satire on government; on the fashion for Austro-Hungarian movies (Lubitsch and Von Stroheim were very popular); on diplomacy and protocol; and finally on war itself. It makes use of innovative techniques which would not be employed for screen comedy until the 1960s. For example Groucho changes military uniform from shot to shot in the battle scenes, mocking the military love of regalia (and the idea of film continuity).

And when we see help coming for the Freedonian army, it comes in the shape of stock shots of stampeding animals, athletes, motorcycle police, and fire engines.

Bert Kalmar and Harry Ruby, who had provided the mainstream story, music, and shtick for *Horse Feathers*, were the chief architects of *Duck Soup*, with additional gags by Nat Perrin and Arthur Sheekman who had become a writing team for the Groucho-Chico failed radio show *Flywheel, Shyster, and Flywheel*. In fact some of the exchanges in *Duck Soup* started life in the radio show – Michael Barson, who recently edited the radio scripts, spotted 15 routines from *Flywheel* in *Duck Soup*. Maxine, Chico's daughter, sheds interesting light on this

creative cannibalism, believing that the Brothers had exhausted their reservoir of 'sure stuff' skits, accumulated since their days on stage, with the completion of *Duck Soup.*

There are several schools of thought on the extent and intent of political satire in *Duck Soup.* The first thinks that it is a pointed attack on European fascism (Groucho, a rank outsider, is the people's choice, outlines, a 'tough-guy' plan in his sung manifesto 'Just Wait till I get Through with it'), with horrifying echoes of the butchery and inept tactics of the 1914-18 war (Groucho shoots his own men, until Zeppo points out his error). Gerald Mast, writing on classic screen comedy, even sees a chilling comic prophecy, in Chico's trial for treason, of the 1936 Stalin show trials.

The second thinks that the film merely satirizes the larger concepts of government and warfare. The final faction thinks that Kalmar and Ruby were simply doing what they knew best; providing the Marx Brothers with an opportunity to ridicule institutions – and that this was simply their most ambitious and timely target.

Whoever is right, the plot of *Duck Soup* (it was originally entitled *Cracked Ice*, but received its nonsense animal title to ally with its predecessors) had developed some way from the original idea of a Ruritanian skit. When *Duck Soup* opens, with echoes of *Animal Crackers*, wealthy widow Mrs Teasdale has informed the bankrupt Freedonian government that her latest loan is on condition that Rufus T Firefly is installed as President.

A gala welcome celebration is held, with Firefly (Groucho) arriving late and insulting his benefactress ('Will you marry me? Did [your husband] leave you any money? Answer the second question first'). He then sings 'Just Wait till I get Through with it,' a kind of rogues' charter in which he proposes to ban dirty jokes, tax cheats, and shoot inconvenient husbands.

Ambassador Trentino (Louis Calhern), the smooth schemer from neighboring Sylvania, plots with dancer Vera Marcal to discredit Groucho and win Mrs Teasdale's affections and her millions for Sylvania. Trentino hires Chicolini (Chico)

41

and Pinkie (Harpo) as spies to dig up some dirt on Groucho, but is driven to distraction by their crazy explanations (on being asked for Firefly's record, Harpo produces a 78 which he shoots down when Trentino throws it away, while Chico awards him a cigar, trapping the Ambassador's fingers in the box). Chico and Harpo conduct an escalating feud with the lemonade-seller (Edgar Kennedy, master of the 'slow-burn,' a technique he had practiced on Laurel and Hardy for McCarey).

Meanwhile, Groucho runs rings round the cabinet:

> MINISTER: How about taking up the tax?
>
> GROUCHO: How about taking up the carpet?

and finally enlists Chico as Minister of War. His hiring is one of their classic nonsense contests, with Chico beating Groucho at his own game:

> GROUCHO: Do you want to be a public nuisance?
>
> CHICO: Sure. How much does it pay?

Bob (Zeppo), Groucho's aide-de-camp, discovers what Trentino is up to, and Groucho goes to Mrs Teasdale's garden party to insult the ambassador, so that he can be thrown out of the country. Their exchange results in a declaration of war, to Mrs Teasdale's horror. That night she calls Groucho over to her house to try and get him to make peace with Trentino. Instead he makes fun of her, ('I can see you right now in the kitchen, bending over a hot stove, but I can't see the stove') and mincemeat of Trentino. Trentino assures Groucho that he is willing to do anything to prevent war. But it is too late; Groucho has paid a month's rent on the battlefield.

Trentino sends his two spies to Mrs Teasdale's where Groucho is staying, having given the war plans to her for safe keeping, Chico and Harpo crash their way through the house, lock Groucho in the bathroom (prompting the immortal line 'Let me out, or throw me a magazine') and impersonate him in cap and nightgown one after another to Mrs Teasdale ('Your dialect is perfect,' she tells a bewilderingly Italian Firefly). Harpo gets the

safe's combination, but uses it on the radio dial, waking the house.

Running away, Harpo smashes a mirror and poses as Groucho's reflection when he comes downstairs. This is one of the all-time great scenes of the Brothers career, even though the routine was as well worn as the hat-swapping Harpo practices on the lemonade-seller. *Variety* ascribed it to the Schwartz Brothers, and it had already appeared in Max Linders film *Seven Years Bad Luck*. Groucho runs through the gamut of tricks to try and fool his 'reflection' but Harpo anticipates his every mood and prop and isn't rumbled till Chico turns up as the third Groucho.

Chico is arrested, charged with treason, and sent for trial. Groucho takes pity on him in court, and starts to mount his defense ('Look at this abject creature,' he tells the court. 'I abject' interjects Chico). Mrs Teasdale interrupts, anxious for a last chance at a peaceful settlement, but Groucho works himself up for an insult, and preempts Trentino. War is declared, and the Four Marx Brothers lead the whole chamber in a wild musical number ('We're Going to War'), complete with minstrel routines, ('They got guns, we got guns, all God's chillun got guns'), square dancing, and banjo playing.

This musical number mixes musical parody – hillbilly and minstrel – with cracks at the Busby Berkeley routines which celebrated war. The 'all God's chillun got guns' mixture of religious and warlike fervor was several years ahead of Chaplin's *The Great Dictator* (1940) and *To Be Or Not To Be* (1942), whose ridicule reflected an existing target in Hitler. Indeed the number's bare-faced bad taste wasn't to be equalled until Mel Brooks created 'Springtime for Hitler' in 1968 for *The Producers*, with its own Busby Berkeley spoof.

Groucho commands Harpo to mount a Paul Revere-type ride through the steets of the capital to announce the war. Typically Harpo is distracted by an undressing blonde. When her husband returns, and goes to take a bath, the mysterious honking sounds from his bathwater announce Harpo's hiding place. Back home, Harpo curls up with his sweetheart – his horse – while his wife sleeps alone.

Villainess Vera Marcal (Mexican firebrand Raquel Torres) gets to grips with President Rufus T Firefly in *Duck Soup*.

On the battlefield, Groucho commands the Freedonian forces (Chico, who is Minister of War, has deserted to the other side). Groucho is armed with a welter of wit (he prescribes two teaspons of soda for a gas attack) but no aptitude for war. He even starts to shoot his own men with a machine gun, and bribes Zeppo to keep quiet when he realizes his mistake. Mrs Teasdale calls from a farmhouse for aid and the four Brothers (Chico has returned – the Freedonian food is better) rush over and fall upon her food.

The situation is desperate, with Sylvanian troops firing on them. Harpo is nominated to get help but he is locked in the ammunition cupboard by mistake which he ignites with a cigarette. When it does come, help is in the shape of track teams, herds of elephants, apes, and fire engines.

Sylvanian troops pour into the farmhouse, but as they are knocked unconscious the last is revealed to be Trentino. He is wedged in the door and pelted with fruit. With his capture, victory is Freedonia's and Mrs Teasdale breaks into an ear-splitting rendition of 'Hail Freedonia.' She is then pelted with fruit herself.

Duck Soup was the last of the Brothers films for Paramount – it had a mixed critical reception and a mediocre effect at the box office. It is the only Marx Brothers film which lacks some sort of love story, and this omission, along with the excision of the musical solos which had been a staple since vaudeville, may have combined with the far-out comedy to alienate audiences.

Furthermore, *Duck Soup* is one of the few films where the Brothers initate and move the plot themselves, rather than reacting or subverting the events of others. Zeppo, for instance, suspects Trentino; Groucho's surreal policies get them into war; and his call to arms makes them victorious. The Marx Brothers were never again to make a film so individual, and McCarey would never make one so anarchic.

Contemporary reviews shed an interesting light on its reception – it's satire either escaped reviewers or disgruntled them. *Photoplay*, for instance, describes it as 'a package of hilarious nonsense that is rib-tickling fun for all who don't care whether their fun has reason in it.' Mordaunt Hall described it in the *New York Times* as 'a production in which the bludgeon is employed more often than the gimlet.'

Leo McCarey, who had mixed memories of his times with the Brothers, and who would never make another anarchic comedy, spoke little of it in later life. The Brothers, who had served up their strongest-ever brew to the public, and been rejected, were offhand about it. Groucho cites the two earliest MGM films as their best in *Groucho and Me*. It wasn't until the Marx Brothers retrospectives of the 1960s that Groucho identified *Duck Soup* as their craziest effort, and credits McCarey as the best director they had.

Duck Soup was integral to the resurgence of interest in the Marx Brothers. European critics had welcomed it in the 1930s, and after enthusiastic essays on both the film and McCarey in *Cahiers du Cinema* in the 1950s, its rehabilitation was complete by 1964. Then French magazine *Telmara* pronounced '*Duck Soup* is 31 years old, and doesn't have a wrinkle. It is the Marx Brothers chef dé oeuvre and one of the greatest comic films in the history of cinema.'

American-audience interest in the film's concerns re-emerged in the antiwar sentiments of the 1960s and early 1970s. The new breed of comedians, whose

BELOW: A publicity still from *Duck Soup*; the film is now regarded as the quintessential Marx Brothers comedy. It was the last time the four brothers appeared together.

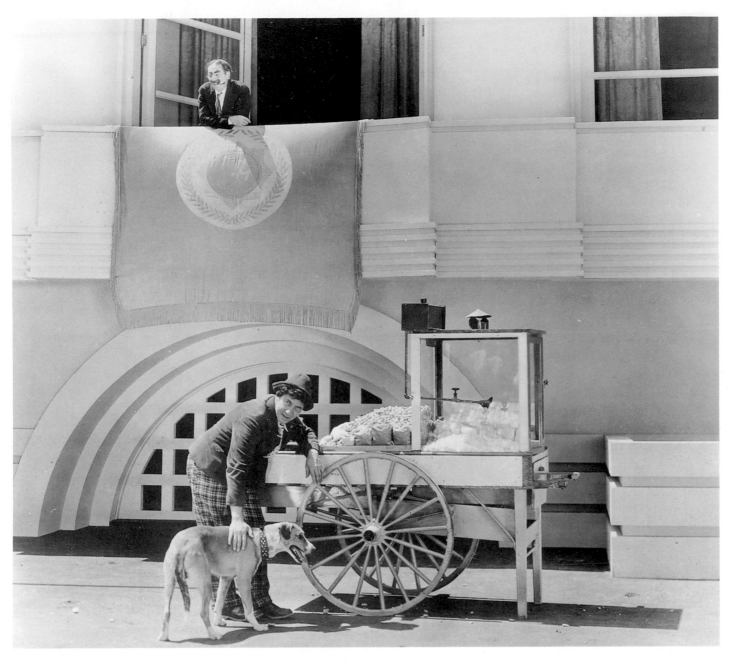

quick-fire saturation comedy was building on foundations provided by the Brothers in the 1930s rediscovered it. Woody Allan lauded it:

> If you were asked to name the best comedies ever made and you named *The Gold Rush, The General* and half a dozen others, *Duck Soup* is the only one that really doesn't have a dull spot.

Duck Soup is nowadays rightfully recognized as the groundbreaking, timeless comedy that it is. Along with *A Night at the Opera* it is one of the Museum of Modern Art's classic choices and is a film repertory staple all over the world. As to whether the auteurists or the anarchists

should carry the day, a *Village Voice* piece in 1991 struck the right balance:

> *Duck Soup* is the Marx Brothers most shapely and intelligent, least cluttery, in a word, best movie. It's no happenstance that it was helmed by the best director who ever worked with the guys.

It might be their most enduring film; it certainly wasn't their most successful. The Marx Brothers motto, 'High pressure, first, last, and always,' in a ruthless, crazy comedy had exhausted their material, lost them their home at Paramount, and cost them their audience. Fortunately, a second chance was just around the corner.

CHAPTER FOUR: **NIGHT AND DAY**

'They've gone about as far as they can go' was the general verdict after *Duck Soup*. For the first time in a hitherto-charmed screen career, which had seen a hit movie a year, by 1934 the Marx Brothers career was becalmed. This year also saw Zeppo's retirement from the act. A letter he wrote to Groucho in March 1934 succinctly outlines his reason: 'I'm sick and tired of being a stooge.'

When Paramount was disinclined to sign them again after the lacklustre box-office performance of *Duck Soup*, it was Chico who found them a new home at MGM. Typically this was through gambling; MGM boy-wonder Irving Thalberg was a bridge crony of his. Thalberg was an object of veneration in a cynical town,

LEFT: The three remaining Marx brothers (minus Zeppo) arrive at MGM with the tools of their trade in 1935.

BELOW: Irving Thalberg, one of Hollywood's youngest movie moguls. He was the model for F Scott Fitzgerald's Monroe Starr in *The Last Tycoon*.

having been Head of Production at Universal Pictures at the age of 21 and of MGM at 25. He was an extraordinary talent with successes like *Ben Hur, Grand Hotel*, and *Mutiny on the Bounty* to his credit. Oddly his name rarely appeared on the credits of his films, as he believed 'If you are in a position to give credit, you don't need it.'

Paramount had been the Brothers' natural home, as the studio had come to specialize in screen comedy: Lubitsch, Mae West, and WC Fields were all on the roster. Thalberg felt that MGM could use some big comic talent in a production slate which was strong on drama, but a new home was going to mean a change in style for The Marx Brothers.

Thalberg insisted on re-appraising the Marx Brothers comedy formula, telling the Brothers that he could get 'twice the box office with half the laughs.' Thalberg's theory was that a more strongly plot-based comedy, with love interest and spectacular musical numbers, would attract a wider audience to their films, building on their already considerable following. The introduction of a love story was to appeal to the female audience, the theory being that they were often alienated by the knowing misogyny of comics like The Marx Brothers and WC Fields.

Thalberg was also keen to plant the gags so that laughs could be timed correctly. He allowed the Brothers to road-test their work in four-city stage tours, where the writers assiduously edited lines according to their reception. This was a device the Brothers had already employed when, years before, Morrie Ryskind sat in the Broadway audience for *Animal Crackers*, deleting any lines which were not a sure thing.

The Brothers' characters were also rounded off to make them more palatable. Groucho made more sense and less

trouble, Chico became smarter, Harpo became more childlike. The MGM films also employ the sort of narrative techniques which apply to comedy drama. The Brothers' fortunes wax and wane in *A Night at the Opera* and *A Day at The Races* in order to win over the audience and allow for a triumphant finale as the lame dogs snatch victory from the jaws of defeat. This is a marked change from the Paramount films which assume a harsher, less realistic world in which everything is fair game and the Brothers are lords of misrule, chasing from joke to joke. If the world is risible, why should we care who wins? The Brothers usually win, but the sudden gag-endings ('I'm looking for a needle in a haystack' says Groucho, tossing hay in *Monkey Business* or pelting the trilling Margaret Dumont with fruit in *Duck Soup*) show how lightly the outcome was taken.

Musically, the MGM films saw a change of emphasis as the baton passed to the young male lead (in these two in-

ABOVE; Lead by Groucho, the three stowaways – disguised as a trio of Russian aviators – receive a hero's welcome.

stances Allan Jones, father of crooner Jack Jones) rather than the satirical songs which featured in the earlier pictures. Songs became the province of romance, rather than comedy, a situation not rectified until Groucho celebrated 'Lydia the Tattooed Lady' in *At the Circus*.

Significantly, the MGM films, although they were enormous hits, are rated less highly by Marx Brothers' enthusiasts. As critic Geoff Andrew puts it, these films were guilty of 'diluting their anarchy with songs and love interest.' This is traditionally laid at Thalberg's door, as the chief architect of their second wave. Interestingly, Hal Roach, veteran Hollywood producer, denied this vehemently in a recent *Time Out* interview:

> Irving knew less about comedy than anyone I ever met . . . He hardly knew they were on the lot, and I guarantee he didn't like them.

Thalberg chose Sam Wood, an excellent, if workmanlike MGM staff director for both *A Night at the Opera* and *A Day at*

the Races, its follow-up. His endless takes drove the Brothers crazy, and there was little love lost between them. 'I can't make an actor out of clay' he raged at them once, earning the response 'And we can't make a director out of Wood.'

The first film to come out of this extensive re-working was to be their most popular ever – *A Night at the Opera*. It established the recipe, identified by Joe Adamson, which would be common to all subsequent MGM Marx Brothers films: an opening scene with Groucho; a friendship struck-up or cemented with the romantic hero by Chico; Chico going several rounds with Groucho. Add a pot pourri of lunacy in a plush setting involving all three Brothers, a fall from grace, and top with a run-amok finale in which all is righted. The screenplay was by Kaufman and Ryskind. Thalberg had been willing to put up the $100,000 it would cost to bring Kaufman to Hollywood by using him on a number of projects.

A Night at the Opera plunges us straight into the plot and the comedy. We

49

see Otis P Driftwood (Groucho) dining back-to-back with the wealthy Mrs Claypool (Margaret Dumont), whom he has promised to introduce into European high society. He introduces her to Mr Gottlieb (a fabulous performance from Lubitsch veteran Siegfried Rumann) who will make her a patron of the opera. Backstage at the opera, villainous star tenor Signor Lassparri (Walter King) is beating Tomasso (Harpo), his dresser, and making unwelcome moves on Rosa (Kitty Carlisle). Her sweetheart Ricardo Baroni (Allan Jones) is a penniless, but talented singer.

Baroni's friend Fiorello (Chico), who has pledged to help him, sells him to Groucho, who has come backstage eager to grab a piece of agent action, looking for 'The greatest tenor in the world.' They all set off for New York for Lassparri's debut, Harpo, Chico, and Ricardo being smuggled aboard in Groucho's trunk.

This first section of the movie has two of the Brothers' most famous scenes; the 'Sanity Clause' contract negotiation between Chico and Groucho and the stateroom stuffed to bursting, both of which

are familiar to people who have never seen the movie. They are preceded by yet another zinger of an opener – concise, with its backstory all neatly presented in one exchange ('Mr Driftwood, three months ago you promised to put me into society. In all that time you've done nothing but draw a handsome salary').

The scene bristles with Groucho's wit and opportunism. Groucho has the same comic ambivalence as ever in his dealings with her. While 'making love to Mrs Claypool is my racket,' he can't help ridiculing the whole process by insulting her and sending himself up ('You'll get into society. Then you can marry me and they'll kick you out of society. And all you'll have lost is two hundred thousand dollars').

LEFT: 'Peanuts!' Groucho turns a fast buck in the stalls in *A Night at the Opera*.

The contract negotiation is probably the finest example of the Groucho-Chico verbal armwrestle, which was retained from their earlier work. It emerges here streamlined, effortless, and with a kind of perverse logic:

GROUCHO: Could he sail tomorrow?

CHICO: You pay him enough money he could sail yesterday.

While the puns have become more sophisticated and less parochial.

GROUCHO: That's what they call a sanity clause.

CHICO: Oh no. You can't fool me. There ain't no Sanity Clause!

And as they shred away at their contracts amiably,

CHICO: I no like the second party.

GROUCHO: Well, you should have come to the first party. We didn't get home till around four in the morning. I was blind for three days.

until they are both no larger than a bookmark, we are treated to a seamless

ABOVE: 'I can't make an actor out of clay.' 'And we can't make a director out of Wood'. Director Sam Wood and his leading men.

RIGHT: 'Tell your Aunt Minnie to send up a bigger room.' The famous stateroom scene from *A Night at the Opera*.

dialogue. Interestingly, this is prefaced by a bizarre sight gag as they use the unconscious body of Lassparri as the rail of an invisible bar. It's a surreal touch straight out of their old style and proves that Thalberg didn't fix what wasn't broken.

The stateroom scene is the visual counterpart of the verbal deftness of the 'Sanity Clause' scene. Groucho, a little put out by discovering that not only does his trunk contain stowaways but also that his stateroom is scarcely larger than his luggage, is greeted by a bewildering succession of shipboard help, who fill the room with maids, cleaners, waiters, boilermen, manicurists, and a hapless woman looking for her Aunt Minnie. What makes this scene even funnier is that the chaos is not of the Brothers' making although they *have* ordered enough food for an army. The waves of help arrive by some cosmic order and the Brothers take it all in their stride ('Tell Aunt Minnie to send up a bigger room') until the arrival of Mrs Claypool causes them to spill out into the corridor.

The second half of the film chronicles their downfall in New York. Harpo steals the beards and uniforms of three celebrated Russian aviators, and, thus disguised, the stowaways disembark to find themselves in a civic reception to welcome the Russians. They are unmasked when Harpo un-gums his beard with a drink of water.

Hiding out in Groucho's hotel suite, the Brothers manage to foil the detective who has tracked them down. This scene is the finest example of the room-to-room runarounds the Brothers had been practicing since the connecting-bedroom antics of *The Cocoanuts*. By rotating the furniture between rooms, until they finally turn themselves into an old couple with a rocking chair (Chico plays the chair) the Brothers manage to lose and confuse the detective completely.

Groucho falls out of favor with Mr Gottlieb and Mrs Claypool, but the quartet gain their triumphant revenge, as they con their way into the opera house, disrupting the opening night *Il Trovatore*. Here we see the first fruit of the marriage of MGM's vast and lavish settings, with the Brothers' genius for destruction. It's a brilliant sequence, with the Brothers

attacking on several fronts. Groucho heckles from the audience while Chico runs rings around the police on stage, Harpo scales the scenery, and the orchestra breaks into 'Take Me Out to the Ballgame' which has been inserted into their sheet music. In the ensuing confusion, by kidnapping Lassparri and holding him hostage in the flies, the Marx Brothers allow Ricardo and Rosa to take the stage for the second act and win over the audience.

The decision to introduce the all-stops-out finale to the Marx Brothers can be counted as one of MGM's successful innovations. It offers a satisfaction to the audience, even if the carefully orchestrated comedy is different from the gag-stream which used to wind-down their Paramount Pictures. One need only contrast the big moves of *A Night at the Opera* with the fisticuffs and bits of business which bring *Monkey Business* to a close, or the end of *Animal Crackers* or *Horse Feathers* to see how much had changed.

ABOVE: Chico and Harpo insert 'Take Me Out to the Ballgame' into the score of *Il Trovatore*.

ABOVE: Allan Jones (father of singer Jack Jones) and Maureen O'Sullivan pose with the Brothers and Margaret Dumont in *A Day at the Races* (1937). Maureen O'Sullivan also has a famous offspring – Mia Farrow.

A Night at the Opera was the Brothers' biggest-ever success at the box office grossing over US$3million in 1935, doubling the take of *Duck Soup*. It marked the high-point of the Brothers' film career to date, (*Duck Soup* didn't garner the recognition it deserved until the Marx Brothers' retrospectives of the 1960s and 1970s). This huge success confirmed the Brothers as the highly popular comedy stars that Thalberg had foreseen. To those who loved their earlier, purely comic capers, it was a mixed blessing in that it confirmed the studio's thinking that this was the recipe to be followed at all costs.

Their 1937 follow-up *A Day at the Races* closely resembles its stable mate in many respects. Groucho again plays a shyster propelled into power by conning a formidable widow – here he is Dr Hugo Z Hackenbush (or as Chico has it, 'Hackenapuss'). Groucho is a horse doctor who is appointed head of a failing sanatorium because of his hold over wealthy hypochondriac Emily Upjohn (Margaret Dumont). Sanatorium retainer Toni (Chico) and hapless jockey Stuffy (Harpo) enlist Groucho's help to aid young lovers Gil Stewart (Allan Jones) and Judy Standish (Maureen O'Sullivan, veteran of several Tarzan movies) keep the sanatorium open. It is under threat from the shifty owner of a nearby racetrack, Mr Morgan (Douglas Dumbrille), who is secretly scheming with the manager Whitmore to add it to his empire.

In an effort to win enough to save the sanatorium, Gil Stewart has sunk his savings in a racehorse, Hi-Hat. The animal hates Morgan, who mistreated him in the past. When Morgan and Whitmore introduce sleazy blonde Miss Marlowe to entrap Groucho, Harpo overhears their plan and he and Chico lay siege to Groucho's bedroom, even as he lays siege to Miss Marlowe. Chico and Harpo save Groucho from discovery by Mrs Upjohn by burying the couple under wallpaper.

They cannot save him, however, when the sanatorium specialists, suspicious of Groucho's abilities, demand that he

53

examine Mrs Upjohn to prove his theory of 'double blood-pressure.' Aided by Chico and Harpo (dressed in garage overalls), their triple examination of Margaret Dumont becomes a combined shave, shoeshine, and three-ring circus and the trio are all thrown out.

Facing disaster, there's nothing for it but a musical number, with Maureen O'Sullivan and Gil Stewart assuring one another that 'Tomorrow is another Day.' Generally the music in *A Day at the Races* is more palatable (probably less light-operatic) than the Kitty Carlisle/Allan Jones duets of *A Night at the Opera*. After the 'character' number – the peasants who were serenaded in the ship's hold of *A Night at the Opera* are here the negro inhabitants of nearby shacks – the sheriff and baddies arrive to break up the party.

Disgraced, the group's last chance is to smuggle Hi-Hat into the next day's big race disguised as another horse. Despite our heroes' attempt at delaying the race (they divert cars on to the track for 'Nice free parking, get your free parking here'), Hi-Hat, ridden by Harpo, joins the race after its start. Ingeniously, the Brothers spur him on to win by using photographs of the hated Margan and by tannoying his voice on to the course whenever Hi-Hat is flagging. The sanatorium is saved, Groucho is reunited with Mrs Upjohn, and the Marx Brothers had another commercial winner on their hands.

A Day at the Races is hugely enjoyable, even if it misses the 'great' status of *A Night at the Opera*. It has been suggested that this is because while the sanatorium fulfilled screenwriter James K McGuiness's maxim that 'the secret of the Marx Brothers is the way they can louse up something dignified,' the racetrack scenes do not.

ABOVE: Harpo and Chico wallpaper Groucho's love-nest in *A Day at the Races*. Note Esther Muir's look of genuine alarm.

In fact it may be more to do with the desire and subsequent enjoyment of putting the Brothers into highly organized settings and watching them take those settings apart. Graham Greene, who was reviewing films during this period, is one of the few critics who rates *A Day at the Races* above *A Night at the Opera*, but even he bemoaned the lavish sets and musical numbers:

> These revellers of a higher idiocy should not mingle with real people nor play before lavish scenery and an arty camera. Like the Elizabethans, they need only a chair.

Some of the finest comedy in *A Day at the Races* is in fact very simple, giving strength to Greene's contention. Look at Groucho having the sanatorium manager in a whirl when the manager speaks to Groucho on the telephone (thinking him to be the Florida Medical Board) seeking Dr Hackenbush's credentials, and Groucho calls him to the intercom as Dr Hackenbush repeatedly so that the manager cannot hear the telephone responses.

The examination scene, in which Chico and Harpo aid Groucho when he is challenged to examine Mrs Upjohn is similarly straightforward. It's a stream of medical sight gags (Harpo and Chico wear mechanics overalls, scrub up maniacally, and dry their hands on one another's coat tails) culminating in a frenzied shoeshine and barber attack on Margaret Dumont. With nowhere to go, the Brothers are rescued by the sprinkler system reducing the room to chaos, allowing them to escape on the racehorse.

The Groucho-Chico exchange has a

BELOW: Groucho and Margaret Dumont in *A Day at the Races.* Hackenbush was Groucho's favorite role; in later life he used Dr Hackenbush as a pseudonym.

slightly different flavor in this instance. Commonly known as the 'Tootsie-fruit-sie' scene, it shows Chico fleecing a wary Groucho, who has come to bet on a cert, but is sidetracked by Chico's hot tip

CHICO: One dollar and you remember me all your life.

GROUCHO: That's the most nauseating proposition I've ever heard.

In order to decode the tip, and then the information in the codebooks that Chico sells him, Groucho buys a succession of books from Chico's ice-cream cart, only to have Chico bet the proceeds of the sale on Groucho's original horse and clean up. Chico himself thought that this was his best scene anywhere in a Marx Brothers film – perhaps because he trounces his brother!

This scene gives us a rare chance to see Groucho and Chico with a hint of low-life about them, an opportunity to see Minnie's boys in something approaching their natural habitat. It has spin and sleaze and we love the way Groucho can see the sting coming but can't (or doesn't want to) get out of the way.

Margaret Dumont won a Best Supporting Actress Oscar for her performance in *A Day at the Races*, which in retrospect seems a long-service medal for her work with the Brothers. Her insights into how they worked on set, reported by co-star Maureen O'Sullivan in a *Screen and Radio Weekly* article of the time, suggests that she may not have been the sweet, dense dowager that the Brothers always made her out to be in real life, as her characters were in the films:

It's rather a proud moment to [the Marx Brothers] when a player laughs during a scene. Then they know the audience will do likewise!

The MGM Marx Brothers' comedies, because of the way comedies have changed, look more old-fashioned nowadays than the Paramount comedies which preceded them. Now that quick-fire saturation comedy is the order of the day, audiences can cope comfortably with the lunacies of *Duck Soup* and *Monkey Business*, and are sometimes bored or, more often, amused for the wrong reasons by the lavish musical numbers which made these films so popular on release. 'Alone,' for instance, may have stayed at the top of the hit parade for 16 weeks in 1936, but just listen to the audience guffaws as Allan Jones steps through the casement window to serenade Kitty Carlisle.

Though the numbers don't have the pep and parody which we associate with the huge MGM musicals of the 1950s – *Singin' in the Rain, An American in Paris* – they are a small price to pay for a pair of movies which were to prove the renaissance of a comedy career which flourished where others faltered. Laurel and Hardy, for example, never recovered from the departure of Hal Roach from MGM, and Buster Keaton was unhappily relaunched by Metro at the same time.

Unfortunately the Marx Brothers'

BELOW: 'Tootsie frootsie ice cream': Groucho asks for a racing tip and acquires a library during *A Day at the Races*.

RIGHT: Chico and Harpo save Groucho from himself (and Esther Muir) in *A Day at the Races*.

comedy renaissance was to be brief. When Thalberg died of pneumonia during pre-production of *At the Races*, the Marx Brothers were left without a patron at the studio. The road tours which were at the heart of their work were abandoned as too expensive, and their longtime writers of choice were also out of bounds. The Brothers could only capitalize on their recent successes by seeking a temporary home elsewhere at RKO.

57

CHAPTER FIVE: **TIMES CHANGE**

LEFT: Chico and Harpo work their double act on Iris Adrian in *Go West* (1940).

BELOW: The Brothers bamboozle innocent author Leo Davis (Frank Albertson) in *Room Service* (1938). A young Lucille Ball looks on.

The augurs were good for *Room Service* as RKO paid a record sum, $225,000, for the Broadway smash as a vehicle for the Brothers. The deal was negotiated by Zeppo, who had set up as an agent, and was to have been the first of a three-picture contract with RKO.

Room Service has a certain curiosity value among the Marx Brothers' films, being the only one which had not been specially written for them, or originated for them as a stage piece. The story structure and characters of the original play were retained, with the Brothers slotted into existing roles, and sequences of Marx Brothers' Mania inserted into the plot.

Morrie Ryskind adapted the play for the screen, and Laurel and Hardy veteran William Seiter (*Sons of the Desert*) directed it.

In complete contrast to the wide-ranging locations and lavish sets of the pair of MGM movies which had preceded it, *Room Service* takes place almost entirely in two hotel rooms. A theater company is hiding out in the hotel while they seek backing for their play in the hotel theater. They have run up a whopping bill. Groucho is the wily producer Gordon Miller, Chico is Harry Binelli, the director of the play, and Harpo Faker Englund. The young Lucille Ball makes an appearance (she was at that time 'Queen of the

Bs' at RKO) as secretary Christine who finds a backer for the show at her day job. Hick author Leo Davis arrives to see his play and the Brothers rope him in with a fake illness to keep the rampaging hotel-chain supervisor from throwing them out.

The hotel takes the backer's cheque as security against the hotel bill and agree to bankroll the show. When the hotel manager discovers that the cheque has been stopped (by the suspicious backer) just as the play is about to start, the Brothers mount a fake suicide to stall him until the play finishes. To delay him further, they mount another; this time, Harpo with a theatrical dagger (his name is, after all, Faker). Surprise surprise, the show (a mining melodrama) is a hit, and Davis can marry his sweetheart, the hotel secretary Hilda.

Room Service drops in dialogue set-pieces for Groucho – his mixture of insolence and nonsense is ever present bamboozling the management and the backers. Chico, making a change from his characteristic aimiable punning, has a nice spread of one-liners. He often gets the line that tops the scene, such as remarking hungrily of a waiter 'I could eat him raw.' Harpo, too, has variations on his usual silent themes; he chases a turkey round their room, breaking it up, and survives a doctor's examination by using a squeaky doll as his mouthpiece.

Room Service, while not up to the standard of its predecessors, manages to hold its own among the later movies. Though often viewed as an unhappy, slow-paced and anomalous chapter in the Brothers' screen career, because it strays from the established format of a Marx Brothers' movie, it has a pleasant black-comedy feel about it. The first act, which is replete with stage-farce mis-understandings, has enough Marx whizz about it to pass muster and the dual suicide high-jinks in the last act are fraught and funny. What lets it down is the supporting cast, who are playing stagily around them. Interestingly the two female roles contain stars in the making, though not on the strength of *Room Service*. Lucille Ball, who was to go on to be possibly the most famous comedienne of the 1950s and 1960s in *I Love*

BELOW: Harpo wins the public approval of a seal in *At the Circus* (1939).

Lucy just reacts pleasantly to the action, and her fellow starlet Ann Miller (no mean comedienne herself in *On The Town* and *Kiss Me Kate*) shows neither the famous legs, nor her customary snap and crackle.

In *Room Service* the Brothers are required to live in the real world, and have a level of responsibility which they have nowhere else in their vagabond screen life. Though they win their backing by deception, their predicament gives it a less careless feel than when they were lending their illogical aid (often more of a hindrance than a help) to young lovers in the MGM movies.

The Brothers themselves were unhappy with this appearance in borrowed clothes; Chico felt that 'It was the first time we had tried doing a play we hadn't created ourselves . . . we can't do that. We've got to originate the characters and situations ourselves.' But as late as 1967 Groucho had mellowed sufficiently to tell a Gallery of Modern Art tribute 'I think it was one of the funniest pictures we made. Very successful.'

The Brothers returned to MGM for *At*

the Circus, the first of a new three-picture contract there for the handsome sum of $250,000 per movie. *At the Circus* continues the trend of later Marx Brothers' films to substitute an event (such as a race-meeting) for the stuffy institutions of the earlier pictures. Thus their work from *A Night at the Opera* onward earns the customary bad rap from Marx Brothers' critics who disparage any setting other than the strictly formal, which will allow the Brothers full reign for their anti-establishment satire.

At the Circus, which must have seemed ripe for joyous anarchy, original production numbers, and big box office, is in reality a pale imitation of its MGM forerunners. What it shares with *At the Races* is the introduction of a setting in which one might logically find the Marx Brothers. Harpo for the first time in his screen career looks quite at home.

The plot centers around the stolen takings of a circus managed by young blueblood Jeff Wilson, played by Kenny Baker. When Chico, playing faithful circus dogsbody Pirelli, discovers that Mr Carter, the circus's owner, is pressurizing

BELOW: 'That's murder, pronounced M O I D E R;' Groucho's J Cheever Loophole interrogates Little Professor Atom in his caravan *At the Circus*.

61

Jeff Wilson to pay the balance owed on the circus, he telegraphs J Cheever Loophole (Groucho) who is listed under 'T' (for trouble) in his address book. When Loophole arrives in torrential rain, Pirelli won't let him on to the circus train without the proper badge ('If you hadn't sent for me, I'd be at home now in a comfortable bed with a hot toddy – that's a drink!')

Onboard the train, Jeff Wilson is knocked out by Goliath the strong man, aided by the midget Professor Atom, and the $10,000 Wilson needs for Carter is stolen. Meanwhile, Groucho is singing 'Lydia the Tatooed Lady' to the circus performers in the buffet. This scene is a wonder in a cramped set; while Groucho skips about and Harpo swings from the light fitting, the circus staff can only sway from side to side. Groucho gives it his all, fittingly as it's one of his most memorable songs, with the sort of satirical lyrics not heard since 'Hooray for Captain Spaulding' (who actually gets a mention here). It has the playful bounce ('Here's Nijinsky doing the rumba. Here's her Social Security Number') which was later to be found with Hope and Crosby in the *Road* movies (when 'like Webster's Dictionary we're Morocco bound').

Groucho is scared off by Goliath, and briskly intimidates and interrogates Professor Atom in his tiny cabin, complete with miniature furniture which Harpo scatters when he sneezes. Carter hides the money with Peerless Pauline, an upside-down-walking novelty artist. Groucho finds and pockets it, but Pauline regains it during a clinch. She hides it in her costume (mutters Groucho: 'I could use the long arm of the law'). He eventually ends up walking on the ceiling with her in the hope that the wallet will fall from her bosom. It does but she runs off with it. Chico and Harpo do a search of the strongman's cabin which recalls their search of Firefly's house in *Duck Soup* – Harpo pulling out a string of visual gags including a sudden impersonation of Santa Claus, in pillow feathers.

When Groucho learns of Jeff Wilson's rich aunt Susannah, (Margaret Dumont, naturally) who can save the circus, he rushes to her mansion to sweet-talk her. It's the same old refrain: 'Oh Susannah, don't you cry for me, oh I need 10,000 dollars for the sheriff's after me!' He tries to stop the French orchestra she has booked for her society party that night so that the circus can take its place. When he fails, Harpo and Chico divert the orchestra to a floating platform, which they then cut loose. The orchestra drifts over the horizon, playing a selection from *Lohengrin*. Jeff's Circus, which has magically set up while Groucho delays the 400 guests at dinner, then takes over as the evening's entertainment, the highlight of which is Margaret Dumont being shot from a cannon. The money is made and the circus is saved.

Despite a handful of high points (the three Brothers' inept interrogation of Professor Atom; 'Lydia the Tatooed Lady') *At the Circus* is an example of how far short a Marx Brothers' movie could fall from their standard-bearing films from earlier in the decade. Nor is it as enjoyable as the often disparaged comedies to come. *At the Circus* dips into average musical comedy – Jeff Wilson serenades, and his beloved's musical horse act – which don't have the verve of numbers in later movies. Moreover, the Brothers wrestle with a script which makes Groucho a repeated failure and Chico a smiling imbecile (he repeatedly gives the game away, foisting cigars on Groucho when he is trying to coax one from the midget as evidence). Harpo, who often comes out better from these less well-tailored later offerings, is his usual sweet self.

At the Circus was released in 1939 and for many fans marks the end of an era. There is some evidence to support the opinion that the Brothers did their best work in the 1930s and were thus shining old light through new windows in the films which followed.

Go West (1940) was their next picture. The Brothers approached, and later viewed it, in a state of extreme cynicism ('The boys at the studio,' wrote Groucho, 'have lined up another turkey for us . . . but I guess it's just as well to get it over with'). This was harsh, for the film is an example of the knockabout, mainstream musical comedy which the Brothers would produce from here on in. Screenwriter Irving Brecher succeeds here where he failed with *At the Circus*. While

RIGHT: Harpo crowd-pleases with strongman Goliath (Nat Pendleton) in MGM's *At the Circus*.

RIGHT: Groucho gets cozy with Margaret Dumont. Fritz Feld disapproves.

these films don't have the timeless anarchy and zaniness of the earlier Paramount films, they are nonetheless head and shoulders above the vast majority of musical comedies which were being turned out by the gross. Viewers approaching them warily are often pleasantly surprised at how enjoyably they bowl along, sandwiching the Brothers in deliciously familiar encounters, between slices of spirited musical comedy.

In this comedy western, Groucho (S Quentin Quayle) is fleeced at the railroad station by the expert maneuvers of two professional idiots (Chico and Harpo as Brothers Rusty and Joseph Panello). At the same moment, cowboy tenor Terry Turner (John Carroll) is persuading the

ABOVE: Harpo takes his job as a pick-pocket literally in *Go West* (1940).

ABOVE: Baubles, bangles, or beads? Groucho attempts to trade with an Indian maid on the reservation in *Go West*.

chase with the villains, during which Harpo is stretched, like an accordion, between two carriages. The Brothers ingeniously strip the train of wood to fuel the engine (a homage to Buster Keaton's *The General*), and win the race to the railroad meeting.

Go West is a thoroughly likeable movie, with enough vintage Marx content to be interesting. But it has also been noted repeatedly that, while the climactic chase is funny, it's funny by numbers and would be just as funny with any number of other comedians of the day.

The critical response was mixed. Most reviewers were happy to note that the best thing about the film was its last sequence, and although none of the reviews shared Groucho's scathing opinion ('*Go West* was one of the worst pictures we made'), the most they could say for the film was that it was better than the previous two pictures.

But *Go West* is not without its moments. There is a giddy stagecoach scene in which the Brothers drive Beecher to a breakdown over the contract. This is matched by a saloon shoot-out which is as good as anything in the earlier movies: Red Baxter pulls a '45,' Harpo pulls a clothes brush; Groucho disrupting the entertainment; and the Brothers stealing drinks as they are slid down the counter. There are set-pieces on the Indian reservation in which Groucho gets a chance to strut his insults and Harpo his harp, and the communal singing in the waggon ('Riding the Range') is particularly appealing and shows momentarily a 'straight' Groucho, strumming his guitar and singing tunefully, and without grimaces.

There is a title card at the start of the film referring to the exhortation by Horace Greeley to 'Go west, young man, go west.' The problem facing Groucho, Chico, and Harpo at the start of a new decade was that they were no longer young. In 1940 all three Brothers were pushing 50. Their careers had spanned the roughhousing antics of vaudeville, the birth of the 'talkies' and the inspired lunacy of their Paramount films. Knockabout comedy was the rage; Abbott and Costello were hard on their heels. It was time to call it quits.

railroad to buy Dead Man's Gulch, a useless piece of land which has been the subject of a long-standing quarrel between his family and that of his fiancée, Eve Wilson.

Prospecting in the Gulch, Chico and Harpo are given the documents to the land as security on a $10 loan to Eve's father Dan Wilson. When a Mr Beecher comes to town to buy the land (he is secretly in league with town baddie, saloon owner Red Baxter), Groucho steps in to bid up the offer on the boy's behalf. His plan to pocket their money is foiled when the baddies take the documents, but refuse to pay for them.

Our heroes decide to blow the saloon safe to get the money for the Wilsons. Chico and Groucho are sidetracked by the wiles of the saloon girls who find them, but Harpo blows the safe and takes the land deed. Desperate to make their own deal with the railroad, the baddies prevent the lovebirds and their saviours from boarding the train out of town.

The story climaxes with a train-top

65

CHAPTER SIX: **FINAL BOWS**

The Marx Brothers had been thinking of retiring for some little time, and once the decision had been taken that *The Big Store* (1941) was to be their last film, they announced their decision in typically zany style; an MGM trailer for the movie has them announcing it to a vast (stock shot) crowd, who protest the decision.

Groucho announced to the Los Angeles *Herald* during production that 'our stuff is simply growing stale. So are we.' New careers were being forged in radio, and Groucho had a yen for radio stardom. Radio was used then as TV is used now: as a stepping-stone to movie stardom (Bob Hope and Bing Crosby both began their careers on radio) or as a home for stars on the wane. So it is with TV today, whence stars spring (Travolta, Cosby) or get their second wind (Candice Bergen in *Murphy Brown*, Burt Reynolds in *Evening Shade*). Radio shows had a multi-million following all through the forties, and the medium's grip didn't loosen until the late 1950s.

The Big Store was taken from an original story by Nat Perrin (Groucho's character, Wolf J Flywheel is a blood brother to the wily Waldorf T Flywheel of their 1932-33 radio series *Flywheel, Shyster and Flywheel* which Perrin co-wrote) and marks a return to some of the staples of earlier Marx Brothers' work.

Singer/composer Tommy Rogers (Tony Martin) saves the music conservatory at which Ravelli (Chico) teaches when he is left half of a department store. When Tommy is attacked in the store, his aunt Martha Phelps (Margaret Dumont, wonderfully skittish and girlish) hires Wolf J Flywheel (Groucho), a seedy detective assisted by the resourceful Wacky (Harpo) to protect Tommy. Little does she know that his assailants are in the pay of her fiancé, the store's manager Mr Grover, who plans to kill Tommy, marry her, and inherit the store. Tommy is in love with Joan Sutton, whose brother is involved in Grover's plans. We know they are in love because he sings to her — happily the song is 'If It's You,' the prettiest and most original love song anywhere in a Marx Brothers' movie, part written by band leader Artie Shaw.

Aided by Chico, who has sworn to protect Tommy, Groucho and Harpo stake out the store. Grover sends a pair of men in gray raincoats to rub out Tommy. However the Hastings Brothers (also a pair of men in gray raincoats) are on their way to a meeting with Tommy to buy his share in the store. Groucho manages to handcuff the wrong pair, before Grover launches a last desperate attack by snatching Joan at a celebration party for the Hastings deal. Chico takes a photograph at the moment Joan is kidnapped and then Grover and his men chase the Marx Brothers all over the store in an attempt to regain the only

LEFT: Marion Martin played a glamorous villainess in *The Big Store* (1941). With this film the Brothers announced their retirement.

BELOW: Margaret Dumont, 'the fifth Marx Brother', made her last appearance with the Brothers in *The Big Store*.

print. The chase involves bicycling, roller skating, unicycling and anything else the Brothers can lay their hands on.

All the best-loved trade Marx are here. Groucho's office introduction to Margaret Dumont while a manic Harpo brings phoney messages, types, and cooks covertly, is vintage stuff; so is his pitch and woo to Martha Phelps.

> MARTHA: But I'm afraid after we're married a while, a beautiful young girl will come along and – you'll forget all about me.
> GROUCHO: Don't be silly. I'll write you twice a week.

Margaret Dumont seems to take to it like a duck to water. Just compare her girlish flutters and give-and-take with the battleaxe matron to whom Groucho laid siege in *The Cocoanuts*.

The musical solos are spirited, with Chico and Harpo engaged in a novelty piano duet together (à la *A Night at the Opera*). And Harpo has a charming dream-like sequence in which he plays, costumed as an eighteenth-Century nobleman, in a string trio with his two mirrored reflexions (a faint nod to the mirror game of *Duck Soup*). Groucho's contribution is 'Sing While You Sell,' a sweeping and rather jumpy swing number, which gathers up the staff and shop-displays in a succession of vignettes.

Among the civilians, Tony Martin's rendition of 'Tenement Symphony,' legendarily loathed by film scholars, has acquired a kind of compulsive camp with time. Who can fail to warm to a song performed by an orchestra of underprivileged children, with lyrics that tell you 'The sounds of the ghetto/inspired the allegretto'?

Chico isn't overextended (he is a faithful friend here, rather than a faithful retainer). While he came out rather well from the much shakier *Room Service* where he displayed a mordant humor and his idiot puns and sunny obstinacy helped carry *At the Circus*, here he is reduced to a good-humored support. Harpo fares better; he retains enough of his old wickedness to hand in Martha Phelps's purse when he finds it but keeps the money.

As in *Go West* the denouement of *The*

Big Store is purely physical comedy, using props available in the department store – message tubes, linoleum rolls, roller skates (remember Harpo being stretched between train carriages or whirled round by a signal). Ingenuity seems to have been sacrificed for physical jerks, an unfortunate trend as the brothers were ageing and have clearly visible doubles for much of the rough stuff. *The Big Store*, with its loveable old gags (Groucho, finishing his morning paper instructs Chico to 'take this paper out and sell it') and cheery production numbers was an aimiable, bouncy, and creditable farewell offering.

Except of course that it wasn't farewell, but au revoir. The Marx Brothers were

ABOVE; Harpo forms a fantasy trio with his own reflections in *The Big Store*.

ABOVE RIGHT: Groucho gets the hump with Chico's cab service in *A Night in Casablanca* (1946).

RIGHT: Harpo entertaining the troops in *Stage Door Canteen* (1943). Other stars making brief appearances were Katharine Hepburn, Edgar Bergen, and Benny Goodman.

gainfully and happily employed throughout the war years. Groucho did radio work, Chico took to the night-club circuit with a dance band ('Chico Marx and His Ravellis'), and Harpo entertained the troops. Harpo not only spoke during these jaunts – better still he joked. When asked if he read Shakespeare, he quipped 'Sure, I read everything of his as it comes out.'

The Brothers were tempted out of retirement with a participation contract for *A Night in Casablanca* (1946), a spoof of the highly successful Bogart/Bergman classic. It wasn't just the participation that motivated them: Chico, whose life-long gambling had left him broke, needed the movie-work. And to get the work, he needed his brothers. Producer David Loew even offered Harpo $55,000 to speak in the movie, which he quite properly refused with a shake of the head.

During production, Groucho got in-

69

LEFT: Chico and Harpo stow away (again) in Sig Rumann's trunk in *A Night in Casablanca*. Harpo's hair (for the first time in his screen career) is his own.

BELOW LEFT: Sleeping on the job – Groucho shows off his novel hotel-management style in *A Night in Casablanca*.

BELOW: Ilona Massey threatens an unperturbed Groucho in *Lova happy* (1949).

volved gratuitously in a long mickey-taking correspondence with Warner Brothers over the title. He claimed that as the Marx Brothers has been professional brothers longer than the Warners, they were fine ones to talk about copyright. In fact, the setting, and the foiling of the Nazis, are all the two movies have in common.

A Night In Casablanca restores Sig Rumann to the Marx Brothers orbit, as an art-loving Nazi Stubel, posing as Count Pfefferman who has bumped off successive managers of the Casablanca Hotel, searching for a hidden art trove. He thrashes his valet Rusty (Harpo) for fooling with his belongings (recalling *A Night at the Opera*).

After vacuuming Stubel's toupee up in revenge, Harpo is challenged to a duel with Karl, Stubel's bodyguard, which he wins by wearing him out. New manager Roger Kornblow (Groucho) arrives, with camel merchant Corbaccio (Chico), and proceeds to play havoc with new rules for the hotel:

GROUCHO: The first thing we're going to do is change all the numbers on the doors.

OWNER: But the guests, they will go into the wrong rooms. Think of the confusion.

GROUCHO: Yeah, but think of the fun.

Vamp Beatrice Rheiner (Lisette Verea) is sent by Stubel to regain his toupee from Groucho's office, and they make a supper date. Chico and Harpo run riot in the club, adding extra tables and chairs for tips. Beatrice tries to trap Groucho into a seduction scene so that Stubel can burst in and shoot him as his rival. But Chico installs himself as Groucho's bodyguard (shades of *Monkey Business*). Chico's attentions ('Hey boss, you got a woman in

there?' 'If I haven't I've been wasting thirty minutes of valuable time'), along with Stubel's menace, force Groucho to lug his mobile romance kit of table, champagne, and flowers around the hotel with Miss Rheiner, only to have her stolen by Chico.

Events come to a head when Harpo discovers the art hoard – while freeing Groucho from a stalled elevator – and Stubel steals it and tries to flee. As he packs, the brothers stealthily unpack for him, finally hiding themselves in the trunks and accompanying him to the airport. Here they stun the plane's crew and replace them in the cabin. Harpo fiddles with the controls, sending the plane taxiing drunkenly, and pilots it into the Casbah, where Stubel is unmasked at police headquarters, and a reformed Beatrice flees the three brothers.

Kalmar and Ruby's best-known song appears in *A Night In Casablanca* – the very famous 'Who's Sorry Now,' though the script was in fact written by Joseph Fields and Roland Kibbee. This followed the MGM policy for later Marx Brothers works of teaming mature performing talent with lesser-known writing talent. Chico and Harpo adopt low- and high-brow musical stances respectively – Chico pounds out the Beer Barrel Polka, where Harpo has the second Hungarian Rhapsody – and Groucho battles gamely with lines which sound like parodies of his most famous work.

There is a strong sense of *déja vu* about the whole thing. It's enjoyable, even prompting the odd laugh out loud on occasions: Harpo is moved on from a building by a cop who sardonically accuses him of holding it up. Harpo walks away – and it collapses. But *A Night In Casablanca*, while proving that the Marx Brothers' know-how still knew how, also suggested that it had had enough. James Agee, writing in *The Nation*, suggested the unthinkable; the Brothers were tired.

Frankly, the major factor bringing them back to work was Chico's need for a steady income – and the fact that the Brothers were established, nay legendary, as a trio but less bankable as individuals. Harpo ran up against this fact when putting together his 1946 film *Love Happy*, which was originally planned to

LEFT: Harpo loves Lucy; Harpo goofing around with Lucille Ball in a 1955 episode of *I Love Lucy*.

BELOW LEFT: Groucho giving in gracefully in *A Girl in Every Port* (1952)

RIGHT: Groucho hosts *You Bet Your Life*.

BELOW: 'The Secret word is . . .' Groucho celebrates nine years of *You Bet Your Life* with his mascot in 1957.

contain cameos for his brothers, which were expanded by the producers when financial needs made an increased Marx quotient necessary.

Love Happy was to be the last film in which all three brothers would appear together. It is unhappily also their poorest picture, a vehicle for Harpo's pantomime talents which was forced to accommodate his brothers. Groucho outlines the plot as Sam Grunion, a private eye who has been trailing the Romanoff diamonds for eleven years.

Harpo picks them up by accident, hidden in a sardine tin, when he is filching food for a starving theater company. The villainous Madame Egilichi (Ilona Massey) who has also sought the diamonds for years, finds Harpo and has him searched and tortured. Predictably, his

pockets are full of bizarre props. He resists all their efforts, calmly eating the apple they place on his head for a William-Tell-style scare. In order to find the diamonds in the theater, Madame Egilichi becomes a backer for the show. Chico, playing dogsbody Faustino the Great, tries to win her, but misinterprets her commands and offers her 1000 tins of anchovies.

Harpo finds the diamonds, but now has the Romanoffs on his case, when they blackmail Sam Grunion into obtaining the diamonds for them. Finally Harpo outwits everyone in a rooftop chase over Times Square, where he plays with the neon signs, then leads the villains up a flagpole and ties them up. He winds up with the jewels, innocent of their value, and Groucho ends up with Madame Egilichi.

The film was not a success, and is very rarely seen nowadays. When the production stalled, producer Lester Cowan was forced to seek extra money by including specific product advertisements in the scene where Harpo gambols on the neon signs. Oddly enough, this blatant sponsorship is part of the only magical scene in the film; Harpo mimicking the sleepy Goodyear boy, riding the Mobilgas horse as a cowboy, hiding in the Kool penguin.

Comedy had changed significantly during the 1940s. The new stars were Abbott and Costello, who combined fast-talking abuse with slapstick clowning. Musical comedy was dominated first by the glossy and exotic *Road* movies with Bob Hope and Bing Crosby, then by Danny Kaye's tongue-twisting antics in the years after the war. The Marx Brothers, along with other long-lived giants of early screen comedy like Mae West and Buster Keaton, had little appeal for the new, younger audience.

So the brothers busied themselves elsewhere during the 1950s. Chico continued to tour with his band, and made the odd TV variety appearance. Harpo was also a favorite TV guest, appearing often in TV spoofs of his most famous routines, notably with Lucille Ball in an *I Love Lucy* homage to the mirror routine in *Duck Soup*. Zeppo had sold out his agency to MCA after the war, and manufactured airplane parts, while Gummo continued as his brothers' agent.

Groucho graced various undistinguished movies such as *A Girl In Every Port*, and *Will Success Spoil Rock Hunter?*, but his real success came in radio, a medium which had toyed with his affections since the early 1930s. By 1947 Groucho's gifts as an ad-libber, displayed in wartime radio broadcasts, had landed him a radio show. Entitled *You Bet Your Life*, it was a quiz show on which Groucho roasted contestants and reigned as a quipping quiz master. Its success was phenomenal, winning him an award as Best Comedian of the Year in 1949. In 1951 the show transferred successfully to television, where it attracted 30 million viewers at its peak, and won him the ultimate accolade of a second cover of *Time* magazine.

You Bet Your Life confirmed Groucho's status as an American institution. Unlike Chico, whose dialect comedy had dated with vaudeville, or Harpo, whose pantomime talents restricted him to guest spots, Groucho's wisecracking allowed him to retain his place in the public eye. He also published – he had been writing since their days on Broadway and published several volumes of autobiography, humorous essays and a selection of his correspondence in *The Groucho Letters*.

As a footnote to their movie career, the Brothers talents were called upon for one

more film. A curiosity entitled *The Story of Mankind*, it was an attempt to portray history through a series of separate cameo appearances by movie stars. Groucho played the man who discovered New York, Chico played a Spanish monk, and Harpo took the role of Sir Isaac Newton.

Chico's worsening health scrapped production of a 1959 TV pilot for a show *Deputy Seraph* involving all three brothers. He died of a heart attack in 1961 and with him died any hope that the Brothers could be reunited for one last glorious outing. Harpo, also afflicted with heart trouble, died in 1964 just after finishing his enchanting autobiography *Harpo Speaks*.

So it was Groucho who witnessed the

TOP: Columbus (Anthony Dexter) demonstrates his navigational theory to the Monk – Chico in his oddest role ever, in *The Story of Mankind* (1957).

ABOVE: Harpo as Sir Isaac Newton in *The Story of Mankind*.

resurgence of interest in their movies in the 1960s and 1970s, just as it had responded to the moods of the 1920s and 1930s. He contributed to retrospectives, laudatory critical studies and accepted awards, including a special posthumous Oscar in 1974 for the Marx Brothers. His son Arthur co-wrote a Broadway play *Minnie's Boys* in 1970, which starred Shelley Winters as the woman dubbed by Alexander Woollcott 'mother of the two-a-day.'

Groucho even took to the stage himself, frail but funny, performing *An Evening with Groucho Marx* to a packed Carnegie Hall in 1972. He lived to see a Chicago TV station achieve its highest ratings ever by running *A Night at the Opera* nightly for a week in 1976.

He died in August 1977, having become a legend in his own lifetime.

ABOVE; Groucho receives a Special Oscar on behalf of his brothers in 1974, accompanied by companion Erin Fleming.

RIGHT: Groucho appearing in a TV production of *The Mikado* (1960).

EPILOGUE

The Marx Brothers, singly or collectively, had achieved success in every single entertainment medium during their lifetimes. They had conquered stage, screen, radio, and television, and their legacy is still with us in the work of the innumerable comedians who have been influenced by their work.

The Marx Brothers were the first comedy act to exploit fully the potential of film. They introduced the idea of zany or surreal humor to a wide audience, resulting in creative offspring as diverse as *Hellzapoppin'* (1942) and *The Goon Show*. Without *Duck Soup* and its anti-war satire, there would have been no *Dr Strangelove*, or *How I Won The War*.

Their saturation comedy style erupted again in the 1960s, in films like *A Hard Days Night*, inspiring TV shows such as *Rowan and Martins Laugh-In*, and *Monty Python's Flying Circus*. The plot of *The Producers*, Mel Brooks's 1968 hit comedy, was first mooted as a story line for The Marx Brothers in the 1930s, and it owes a great deal to their work. Max Bialystock's toast to success 'wine, women and song – and women' has a familiar ring to it. So does his aggressive nonsense conversation with his partner, the timid Leo Bloom ('So you're an accountant eh, so account for yourself. Do you believe in God? Do you believe in Gold?)

On this specific level Groucho's portrayal of the fast-talking-loser-as-hero paved the way for Bob Hope, Ernie Kovacs (who also sported the cigar), and, ultimately, Woody Allen. Until recently, his best-known acolyte was Hawkeye (Alan Alda rather than Donald Sutherland) in the long-running TV series *M*A*S*H*, whose leers and wisecracks were pure Groucho.

The no-holds-barred approach which the Marx Brothers pioneered is still with

BELOW: Mrs Marx didn't raise any quitters; The Marx Brothers look lively and show a leg.

us today on screen. The genre spoofs *Airplane!* and *The Naked Gun*, with their blithe disregard for verbal or visual logic have their roots in the Marx Brothers' Paramount comedies.

Woody Allen, who is one of the Brothers' greatest fans, has acknowledged their influence on his early films.

And he also summed up what it is that makes The Marx Brothers so timeless. There is a pivotal moment in *Hannah and Her Sisters* when his suicidal hero, Mickey, goes to a showing of *Duck Soup*:

I'm watching these people up on the screen and I started getting hooked

on the film . . . I mean, look at all the people up there on the screen, you know, they're real funny . . . and what if the worst *is* true? What if there's no God and you only go around once and that's it? Well, don't you want to be *part* of the experience? . . . You know, it's not *all* a drag . . . Just enjoy it while it lasts.

This is the Marx Brothers' legacy. For as long as there is an audience for comedy, the Marx Brothers will be immortal. In their world, nothing is sacred except laughter.

ABOVE: (left to right) Monty Python's Graham Chapman, Michael Palin, and Eric Idle; their brand of saturation comedy owes a huge debt to the Marx Brothers.

RIGHT: *At the Circus*; producer Mervyn Le Roy was better known as the director of *Little Caesar* and, later, *Random Harvest*.

LEFT: Gene Wilder and Zero Mostel are reluctant Nazis in *The Producers* (1968). The storyline was mooted as a Marx movie in the 1930s.

RIGHT: Wayne Rogers (Trapper John), Alan Alda (Hawkeye), and Maclean Stevenson horse around in TV's *M*A*S*H*. Alda gave his role more than a little Groucho.

INDEX

Figures in *italics* refer
to illustrations

Abbott and Costello
    65, 73-74
Alda, Alan 76, *79*
Allen, Woody 45, 76
Animal Crackers, stage
    show 2, 25, 26 31, 47
Animal Crackers
    (1930) *4, 14,* 22, 26,
    26, 27, *27,* 31, 34, 37,
    41, 52
At the Circus (1939) *2,*
    5, 22, 49, *60,* 61-62,
    61, 63, 68, *79*

Ball, Lucille 59, 60, *59,*
    61, *72,* 74
Berlin, Irving 23
Big Store, The (1941) *2,*
    66, 67-68, *67, 68*
Broadway 14, 23, 24,
    25, 27, 47, 75
Brooks, Mel 42, 76

Calhern, Louis *11,* 41
Carlisle, Kitty *48,* 50,
    54, 56
Chaplin, Charles 7, 39,
    42
Cocoanuts, The, stage
    show 23-25, 31
Cocoanuts, The, (1930)
    10, *24,* 25, *25,* 26, 37,
    52, 68
comedians and the
    influence of Marx
    Brothers on 76-78
Crosby, Bing 62, 67, 74

Day at the Races, A
    (1934) *3, 13, 15,* 48,
    49, 53-56, *53, 54, 55,*
    56, 57, *57*
deaths of Marx
    Brothers 74, 75
Deputy Seraph, The,
    TV pilot (1959) 74
Duck Soup (1933) 2, 7,
    11, 22, 31, 33, 37, *38,*
    39-45, *39-41, 43-45,*
    47, 48, 53, 56, 62,
    74, 76, 77
Dumont, Margaret *2,*
    24, *26,* 48, 50, 53,
    53, 54, 55, *55,* 56,
    62, *63,* 67, *67,* 68

*Evening with Groucho
    Marx, An,* stage
    show 75

Fields, WC 20, 47
films, influence of
    Marx Brothers on
    76-78, *78-79*
*Flywheel, Shyster and
    Flywheel,* radio
    series 37, 40, 67
Four Nightingales,
    The, vaudeville act
    5, 18, *19, 21*
'Fun in Hi Skule', skit
    19-20, 34

General, The (1962) *39,*
    65
Girl in Every Port, A
    (1952) *72,* 74
Go West (1940) *3, 58,*
    62, 64-65, *64, 65,* 68
Grauman's Chinese
    Theater *37*
Greene, Graham 55

Heerman, Victor 26
'Home Again', skit 22
Hope, Bob 62, 67, 74,
    76
Horse Feathers (1932)
    10, 29, 33-34, *33, 35,*
    36, 37, 40, 52
Humorisk (1920) 25

'I'll Say She Is', revue
    23, 29
I Love Lucy, TV series
    60-61, *72,* 74

Johnstone, Will B 29,
    33
Jones, Allan 49, 50, 53,
    53, 54, 56

Kalmar, Bert 25, 33,
    34, 40, 41, 72
Kaufman, George S 23,
    24, 25, 49
Keaton, Buster 7, 39,
    56, 65, 74

Laurel and Hardy 7,
    27, 39, 42, 56, 59
Levin, Leo 18, *19, 21*
Love Happy (1949) *71,*
    72-73
Lubitsch, Ernst 39, 40,
    47, 50

McCarey, Leo 39, 42,
    44
MacLeod, Norman 30,
    33
Mankiewicz, Herman
    30

Martin, Tony 67, 68
Marx, Gummo, brother
    and agent *1,* 17, 18,
    19, 220, *21,* 22, *22,*
    74
Marx, Minnie, mother
    and agent *16,* 17-18,
    26
Marx, Sam, father 17,
    18, 29
*M*A*S*H,* TV series
    76, *79*
MGM *12,* 44, *46,* 47,
    48, 49, 52, 56, 59, 61,
    67, 72
Mickey's Polo Team
    (1936) 7
Mikado, The, TV
    version (1960) *75*
Minnie's Boys, play
    (1970) 75
Monkey Business
    (1931) *2, 28,* 29-31,
    30-32, 33, 37, 48, 52,
    56
*Monty Python's Flying
    Circus,* TV series 76,
    78
Muir, Esther *15, 54, 57*

Night at the Opera, A
    (1935) *4, 6, 7, 13,* 26,
    33, 45, 48, *48-52,*
    49-53, 54, 55, 61, 68,
    75
Night in Casablanca, A
    (1946) 69, *69, 70,*
    71-72

'On the Mezzanine
    Floor', act 22
Oscars 56, 75, *75*
O'Sullivan, Maureen
    53, *53,* 54, 56

Paramount 10, 25, 26,
    27, *28,* 29, *29,* 37,
    39, 43, 45, 47, 48,
    52, 56, m64, 65, 77
Perelman, SJ 29, 30,
    30, 33
Perrin, Nat 29, 40, 67
Producers, The (1967)
    42, 76, *78*
Pusey, J Carver 29-30

radio shows 37, 40, 67,
    69, 74
RKO 57, 59, 60
Roach, Hal 39, 49, 56
Room Service (1938)
    15, 59-61, *59,* 68
Ruby, Harry 25, 33, 34,
    40, 41, 72
Rumann, Sig *4, 13,* 48,
    50, 71
Ryskind, Morris 23,
    47, 49, 59

Shean, Al, uncle 18,
    20, 22, *22,* 34
Sheekman, Arthur 29,
    40
Stage Door Canteen
    (1934) *69*
stage shows 2, 22, 23-
    25, 26, 29, 31, 47, 75
Story of Mankind, The
    (1957) 74, *74*
Street Cinderella, The,
    stage show 22

Thalberg, Irving 47, *47,*
    49, 52, 53, 57

Todd, Thelma *32, 33,*
    34, 37

vaudeville *5,* 18-20,
    19-21, 23, 26, 29, 65

Wood, Sam 49, *51*
Woollcott, Alexander
    14, 23, *23,* 75

You Bet Your Life,
    radio and TV series
    73, 74

ACKNOWLEDGMENTS

The publisher would like to thank Ron Callow
of Design 23 who designed this book, Liz
Montgomery, the picture researcher, and
Aileen Reid, the editor. We would also like to
thank the following agencies and institutions
who supplied the illustrations:

The Bettmann Archive: pages 12 (above),
14-15, 22 (above), 24 (above), 25, 30 (below),
33, 35 (below), 37, 42-43, 44, 48 (below), 50,
51, 61, 63 (below), 64, 65, 72 (below), 73
(below)

BPL: pages 2 (all five), 3 (both), 4 (above), 5
(below), 6, 7, 10, 11 (below), 13 (both), 14, 15
(above), 26, 30 (above), 32 (both), 35 (above),
36 (above), 40, 41, 45, 46, 47, 48 (above),
50-51, 54, 56-57, 59, 60, 66, 68, 69 (both), 70
(both), 71, 72 (above), 73 (above), 76-77, 78
(both)

Springer/Bettmann Film Archive: pages 1, 4
(both), 5 (above), 12 (below), 17, 20, 21, 22
(below), 27, 31, 36 (below), 38, 52, 53, 57, 58,
63 (above), 67, 74 (both)

**Theater Collection, Museum of the City of
New York:** page 24 (below)

UPI/Bettmann: pages 16, 18, 19, 23, 75 (both)